All Name Index

to

1788

HISTORY

OF

ONTARIO CO.,

NEW YORK,

PHILADELPHIA:
EVERTS, ENSIGN & EVERTS,
716 FILBERT STREET.

1876

by

Mary Loeper Colf, John I. Loeper
and Ruth Nightingale

Heart of the Lakes Publishing
Interlaken, New York

ISBN: 0-932334-81-4
Manfactured in the United States of America

A *quality* publication from
Heart of the Lakes Publishing
Interlaken, New York 14847

A

ABBEY f-80, 106
  Aaron 226
  Anna 246
  Cheney 232
  D. 127
  David 129
  Elizabeth Baker 226
  H. P. 231
  Hiram 250
  I. J. f-225
  Isaac 226
  Jet 59
  John f-80, 108, 226
  Joshua 228, 262
  Lyman 262
  Samuel 79
ABBY
  Samuel 104
ABBOT 119, 199
  Israel 201
  T. L. 124
  William 166
ABEEL 133–4
  Augustus 134
ABEL
  Clement 139
ABERCROMBIE 96
ABERNATHY
  Caleb 163–4
ACADEMY P. O. 120
ACADEMY TRACT 119
ACKER
  David 143–4
ACKLES
  James 160
ACKLEY 43
  Aaron 117
  Asa 254
  Benjamin 108, 124
  C. B. 108
  H. 108
  Harrison 109
  H. 108
  Harrison 109
  Jesse 117
  Olive 203
  Oliver 136, 242
  Pliny 254
  Stephen 192
  William 121, 254
  Zachariah 254
ADAIR
  Emily 146
ADAMS 17–8, 24, 74, 88, 102, 136, 203, 207–9,
    219, 258
  A. 198, 208
  Abigail 211
  Abner 206, 209, 211–2, 214, 230
  Abria 235
  Alden 225
  Alvin 208
  Charles 143, 212
  Chloe 211
  Cyrene Phillips 235
  D. 257
  E. 127
  Edward 211, 213
  G. 191, 200
  Gabriel 257
  Hiram 226
  Humphrey 256
  Isaac 19, 225, 228

ADAMS (cont.)
  J. Q. 33
  James 256
  Jasper 74
  Jno. 124
  John 16–7, 119, 143, 161, 206, 208, 209,
    211–2, 215
  Jonathan 206, 208, 211–2
  Joseph 206, 209, 255
  Julia 212
  Laura 34, 207
  Lucinda 211
  Myron 49, 209, 211–3
  Newton 211
  O. 212, 229
  Oliver 229, 232
  Oscar 213
  Prudence 242
  R. C. 124
  Robert 243
  Rodney & Son 67
  Sarah 201
  Sylvester 195
  W. 127, 201
  William 38, 49, 56, 63, 121, 129, 206,
    208–9
ADAMSON
  James 147
ADGATE
  Caroline 167
ADJUTANT 29
ADSIT
  Charles 171
  Samuel 113
AESCULAPIUS 147
AFFLECT 129
  D. 133
AGARD
  Harnson 266
  William 266
AGAYENTAH 136–7
AIKINS
  John 90
AILSWORTH
  R. 169
AINSLEY
  James 156
  Marvin 143
AINSWORTH 181
  S. H. 49
  Stephen 52, 220, 224
AKEN
  David 226
  Orry 226
  Uriel 226
AKENS
  Charles 120
AKIN
  Alexander 163
  Orra 232
  Uriel 232
AKINS
  David 232
  John 124
ALABASTER
  J. 112–3
ALBAUGH
  Isaac 171
  John 171
ALBERT 230
ALBRIDGE
  Abram 60
ALCOCK
  William 130

ALCOTT
  Harvey 267
ALDERNEY 50
ALDRICH 89, 113, 189
  A. 166, 192
  Ahez 193
  Asa 194
  Brice 19
  C. S. 81, 88, 121
  Charles 110
  Clarkson 190
  David 159, 177
  Edmond 161
  Essick 190
  Francis 182, 195
  Harris 194
  Hiram 176, 182
  Jesse 190, 194
  Lyman 195
  Marcy 193
  Martin 193
  Mason 182
  Myron 196
  N. 194
  Nathan 17, 19, 25, 176, 178, 189, 190,
    193
  Seth 108, 110
  Seymour 115
  Stephen 63, 191–2, 194
  Turner 192–3
  Uriah 190
  William 176, 196
  Willise 190
ALEXANDER
  George 248, 250
  Henry 97
  John 143
ALFORD 44
  Ashley 241
  Homer 248, 250
ALGER
  Benjamin 219
  George 253
  John 219, 255
  Josiah 219
  Samuel 219
ALGONQUIN 9
ALGUR
  John 18, 216
ALLEN 42, 88, 167, 232
  A. C. 59
  C. 219
  Charles f-172
  Chauncey 241
  D. 127, 247–8
  Daniel 192
  David 231
  E. H. 240
  Ebenezer 25
  Edna f-172
  Eli 35, 247–8
  Elias 247
  Frederick 112
  G. C. 129
  Henry 57
  Ira 232
  James 122, 243
  John 143, 221, 247
  Jonas 49, 201
  Jonathan 247
  Joseph 240, 251
  Lester 124
  Levi 243
  M. 113

ALLEN (cont.)
Marvin 113
Matthew 18
Moses 227
N. 231–2
Nathan 241, 247
Nathaniel 37, 49, 52–3, 130, 227, 230–2, f-235
Oliver 223
Orin 139
Orsamus 113, 122
P. 129
Peter 36, 52, 228, 230–2
Polly 241
Robert 205
S. 113, 229
Samuel 169
Solomon 264
T. 127
Theophilus 18, 114, 241, 247–8
Thomas 124
Timothy 129, 180
Wilson and Allen 176, 178–9
ALLENS 248
ALLISON
William 160
ALLYN PARK 129
ALMY
J. S. 257
ALSOP
Thomas 88
ALVERSON
Daniel 112
J. B. 169–70
John 171
Kezia 170
AMBLER
S. F. 109
AMBROSE
Ira 256
AMELIA
Antonia 182
AMERMAN
Frederick 158
AMES
John 243
AMSDEN
Elihu 147
Isaac 145
Joel 160
Laura 148
Simeon 146
ANABEL
& Snyder 179
ANABLE
Charles 124
ANDERSON 132
Aloin 259
Alvin 257
Andrew 139
Daniel 203, 221
Ed. 108
Edwin 123
Emery 259
Francis 120, 234
G. B. 108
George 105
J. C. 167
Jacob 182
James 255, 259
John 124
Joseh 196
Orrin 255, 259
William 142

ANDREWS 232
Albert 121
Benjamin 240
Cornelius 109
Elkanah 53, 242–3
Francis 243
George 238, 240
Harris 115
Heman 115
Joel 104
John 103
S. F. 109
Samuel 112, 240
Sarah 113, 242
ANDRUS FARM 258
ANDRUS
Marcy:139
ANDRUSS 256
George 256
ANGEL
Edwin 147
Jason 160
ANGELO
Louis 142
ANGEVINE
William 182
ANNIN 165
J. 127
Joseph 19, 21, 35, 129, 165
ANSLEY
George 139
ANSON
Silas 160
ANTIS 17, 105, 107
Abner 108
Henry 122
Morse & Phelps 105
Morse & Pierce 105
Rober 112
William f-94, 102–5, 107, 109
ANTHONY
S. N. 64, 129, 131, 133
Simon 195
Susan 103
ANTISDALE 109, 110
Luther 53
Perez 193
APPLETON
R. 208
Richard 120, 243
Richmond 233
ARCHER FARM 249
ARCHER
Benjamin 139
D. C. 187
Dennis 179
G. L. 160
Henry 161
J. W. 160
Jonathan 193
ARCHIBALD
William 266
ARGESTAIGE
George 124
ARLING
Joseph 157
ARMINGTON
Benj. 182
ARMITAGE 179
J. B. 218
John 221
ARMS
Irving 139
ARMSTRONG 17

ARMSTRONG (cont.)
Aden 192
Archibald 152
Arnold 124
Asel 182
David 258
Harry 255, 259
Henry 144, 256
Hiram 131
Oliver 256
Perry 255
Robert 256, 258–9
Walling 256
ARNOLD 156, 180, 217, 258
Betsy f-189
Bushnell 217
Caleb 228–9, 232
Charles 160
Daniel 53, f-189, 190, 193, 196
George 142
Giles 199
H. 194
J. T. 113, 232
Jonathan 154
Pardon 193, 196
William 123, 219, 228
ARTHUS
William, Jr. 96
ASBURY 113, 169–70
ASHBY
Noah 231
ASHLEY 228
Daniel 52, 217
Eliza 225, 236
Frank 226
Hiram 49, 52, 225–6, 236
J. 108
John 206
Minerva f-228, 236
Noah 225–6, f-228, 230–1, 236
Sheldon 254
Tisdale 227
William 226
ASHWORTH 265
ASTOR
John Jacob 16
ATCHINSON 221
ATCHISON 156
B. 156
Henry 248
Sylvester 262
ATKINS
T. 131
ATWATER 24, 26, 49, 104, 106–7, 190
F. 107
Freeman 54, 102–3, 106
Jeremiah 63, 102, 107
Lucius 139
M. 107, 111
Moses 17, 19, 23, 25, 32, 34, 38–40, 42, 44–6, 48–9, 51, 55, 63–4, 78–80, 102–3, 106–7, 110–1, 114, 154
ATWELL
Peter 119
Winthrop 67
ATWOOD 132
Root & So. 50
Edwin 143
George 132
I. M. 182
AUGUR 95
AUKEN
David 165

AUSTIN
A. W. 257
Alanson 254
Charless 214
H. W. 143
J. M. 136, 203
James 79, 154, 240
Jonas 139, 144
Levi 18, 248
Nathaniel 254
Oscar 124
Sylvester 49, 52, 254
AUSTION
N. G. 256
AUSTRY
Arnold 124
AVERILL 97
John 180
AVERY
Joseph 220
AYER
Baley 219
AXTELL 112, 132, 148
Daniel 148
Henry 34, 132, 155, 148
M. 115
William 110
AYER
Oliver 132, 211
AYLWORTH
Levi 53
AYRAULT
Nicholas 69
Walter 75-6, 111
AYRES
Bailey 217
D. M. C. 157
J. M. 157
Job 194
John 217
Lewis 157

B

BABCOCK
E. P. 264
Harrison 234, 259
Hiram 182
Lemuel 160
Myron 157
O. W. 243
Oliver 152, 159
Warder 218
William 113, 159
BABCOCKS
George 18
Isaiah 18
Lemuel 18
William 18
BACHELOR
& Leary 199
BACKENSTOSE
D. B. 130
Edwin 144
Jacob 136
Joseph 136
BACKERSTOSE
E. 83
BACON 16, 17, 206-7
Calvin 34
Chauncy 157
Christopher 171
J. W. 108

BACON (cont.)
P. 227
Philip 233
Tract 116
William 116, 118-9, 206, 209
BADGER
Herber243
Joseph 259, 265
BADGRO
Catherine 254
David 254, 257, 259
John 257
BADGROW
William 55
BAGGERLY 181
Alpheus 179
America 179
Charles 171
Charlotte 179
Everett 179
Gideon 181
Harrison 179
Henry 179
Hezekiah 179, 181
John 60, 165, 169, 179, 181
Peter 60, 161, 181
Robert 181
Samuel 165, 179
Tyson 179
BAGLEY
Jenks 258
BAILEY 129
C. 255
Charles 143-4, 182
E. 242, 256
Elmer 259
Frank 209
George 139, 242
Henry 143,
J. W. 243
James 124
Joel 258
Joseph 259
Richard 135, 156
William 208
Zadoc 30
Zadcock 209, 212
BAINBRIDGE
Darwin 171
William 171
BAIRD
D. W. 130
Thomas 139
W. H. 85, 90
William 139, 144
BAKER 17, 160, 217
A. S. 170
Alexander 157
Ami 263
Anna 226
Apollos 160
Bayze 49, 216-7, 221
Curtis 223
D. J. 118
Daniel 221
Elisha 226
Fred 166
George 221
H. 170
James 169, 223, 226
Jesse 223
John 142-4
Lucy 221
Marvin 218

BAKER (cont.)
Miles 160, 182
O. 218
Ortes 223
Roswell 130
Sarepta 170
Thomas 113
Timothy 176
W. M. 144
William 189, 226, 231-2
BALCH
James 67
BALCOM 178
Asel 160
Columbus 124
Constant 160
Espenetas 160
Phoebe 113
BALDWIN
A. G. 61
Amos 68, 135
Charles 251
Layton 171
G. 154
Nathaniel 207
Robert 257
BALL 103, 119
Charles 157-8, 199
Cyrus 205
Jonathan 218
Lewis 222
BALLARD
Jesse 255
Marin 143
BANCROFT
Albert 88, 182, 243
Conrad 122
W. J. Corp. 100
William 182
BANKS 90, 196
N. P. 95-6, 98
BANNISTER
Caleb 167, 170
Christopher 171
Eli 130
Elizabeth 168
Lemuel 164, 168
T. O. 171
Thaddeus 171
Theodore 164-5
BANTA
Charles 171
BAPPLE
S. 249
BARBER
Amos 241
C. F. V. 256, 259
Daniel 186
Lemuel 263-4
Matthew 213
John 263
Rachael 169
Scott 213
Virgil 68
William 200
Zaccheus 262-3
BARDEN
Chauncey 147
George 124
H. V. f-144
Henry 268
James 139
Luther 139
Otis 147

BARDEN (cont.)
S. P. Levi 147
BARDENT
Tillson 157
BARGDURF
J. C. 265
BARKER
Charles 268
Edward 268
George 144, 171, 268
William 77, 162
BARKLEY
Thomas 181, 230, 232
BARLOW 92, 111
Abner 17, 38, 40, 47–9, 55, 102–3, 106, 112,
114, 117, 126, 262
H. L. 168
J. 166
Nathan 44, 178, 180–1
William 41, 111, 113
BARKSDALE 85, 90–1
BARLEY
W. 216
BARMOUR
Allen 201
BARNARD 257
Abby 236
Chauncey 236
Cynthia 236
Daniel 39
Elizabeth 236
Ellen 236
Fannie 236
Fitch 236
Foster 128, 136
Frances 236
Nancy 236
Percis 225
Peter 236, 259
Robert 148
Samuel 236
Thomas 115
BARNES
A. 192
Daniel 169
David 120, 139
Edward 139
Elias 139
Frederick 139
I. J. 248
Ira 233
James 115, 182
John 30, 206
Rachel 211
Silas 119, 202
W. B. 96
William 182
BARNET
Thomas 205
BARNETT
Edwin 205
BARNEY
Benjamin 176
Charles 143
J. 258
BARNHART
James 200
Joseph: 223, 255
William 182, 218, 223
BARNS
James 139
Barnum 38
John 251
Lewis 221

BARNS (cont.)
T. S. 67
Thomas 66
William 50
BARR
Archibald 144, 171
Oliver 259
BARRETT 208
Catharine 221
David 201
Enoch 205
G. W. 84
John 92, 233
Lyman 264
William 122, 251
BARRINGER
E. 242
John 222
Mercy 240
BARRIS
Edwin 120
BARRON
David 146, f-146, 149, 150
George 150
John 150
Martha 150
Mary 150
Sarah f-146
BARRY
David 158
George 171
BARTHOLOMEW
Thomas 203
William 268
BARTLE 129
BARTLES
James 124
BATES 24, 37, 88, 116
David 75
Esther 112
Frank 116
John 49, 108
Naomi 112
P. O. 53, 56, 111
Phineas 17, 40, 45, 52–4, 58, 79, 102, 106,
112, 115, 176, 193
S. 53
Stephen 29, 51, 53, 58, 79, 102, 106, 117
BARTLETT 136, 259
Alfred 121
Buell 53
Orson 130
BARTON 32
B. 127
Benjamin 12, 16, 21, 32, 53
Jared 198
BARTRAND
B. 255
BASCOM 153
Elias 120
BASE
Samuel 142
BASHFORD 257
John 257
S. 257
Samuel 257–8
BASSET
Richard 92
BASSETT
George 220
Samuel 243
William 154
BATCHELLOR
Charles 233

BATCHELLOR (cont.)
Fayette 232, 234
Wesley 234
BATEMAN
M. B. 144
Martin 171
Richard 171
BATTLES
Joseph 263
BATTY
Talcott & 192
Jonathan 192
BAUM 211
Henry 203, 211
BAXTER
Joseph 33
N. H. 139
Thomas 143–4
BAYARD
Samuel 57
BAYLE
Anthony 124
BAYLES
Charles 243
BAYLESS 169, 171
BAYLEY 129
Alonzo 120
Frank 112
Richard 129
BAYLIS
B. F. 243
BAYNE
Frederick 182
BEACH 68, 199, 207
Alfred 111
Amos 111
Ashbel 18, 209–10
Charles 182
Chauncey 207
David 159
E. 209
Edna 159
Elias 130
Elisha 207, 209
Frances 236
George 213
Israel 209–10
James 182
Jonathan 104
Lavina 139
Lucy 159
Michael 142
Messr. 55
R. B. 131
Richmond 236
Thomas 199, 202
W. B. 265
William 144
BEAL
F. W. 109
BEALE
Archibald 182
BEALS 103
Abigail 112
H. Channing 80
John 104, 107
Johnson & Tiffany 104
Lott 182
Thomas 32, 37–8, 40, 45, 49, 58, 79, 80, 102,
104, 106, 108, 112
BEAL'S LOT 109
BEAM
D. S. 258
D. W. 257

BEAN 129
BEARD 112
   James 171
BEARDSLEY
   Daniel 258
   Jonas 259
   W. 220
BEARMORE
   Nathaniel 258
BEARY
   Jack 238
BEATTIE
   Adam 139
   James 147, 149
BEAUMONT 146
BEAVER
   J. M. 203
BECHER
   John 228
BECKENSTOSE
   Jacob 129
BECKER
   A. B. 257
   George 139
   John 256, 258
BECKET
   Joseph 55
BECKMAN
   H. 127
BECKWITH
   Berrick 192
BECKWORTH
   Andrew 258
BECRAFT 257
BEDDLECOME
   Chas. 195
BEDELL
   Ambrose 139
BEEBE
   A. M. 219
   Allen 214
   Arsino 119
   Ashman 207
   George 223
   Harlow 223
   Heman 207
   Jonathan 119
   L. N. 110
   Levi 112, 119
   Levin 110
   Nancy 110
   Robert 163
   Samuel 211
BEEBEE
   Charles 182
BEECHER
   W. D. 228
BEEKER
   Henry 139
BEEKMAN
   H. 127
BEEMAN 114, 249
   Elam 122
   Gideon 248
   Henry 108
   M. 108, 109
   Marvin 109
   Nelson 248
   W. 118, 119
BEERS
   Fernando 213, 243
   L. D. 254, 257
   Nathan 255, 257

BELCHER
   Edwin 233
BELDING
   Alice 214
   Clarissa 148
   Henry 182
   Merritt 120
BELDNEY 167
BELGER
   Battery 93
   Edwin 124
BELKNAP 248
   John 88
   Jonas 230-1, 263
BELL
   John 171
   Robert 161
   William 124
BELL'S POINT 119, 120
BELL'S TAVERN 129
BEMENT
   Anna 177
   Bradford 171
   Dewey 199
   E. 199
   Ebenezer 199, 202
   Edwin 202
   H. 201
   Harvey 199
   Henry 124, 202
   John 132
   Titus 181
   William 176, 182
BEMGAN
   Martin 157
BEMIS 38, 103, 227
   Block 105
   George 52, 66, 96, 108
   J. D. 49, 107
   J. D. & Co. 64
   James 26, 33, 41, 49, 56, 66, 76, 80, 109–10,
      177, 256
BENEDICT 119
   Gould 251
   John 156
   Robert 118
   Thompson & 104
   William 157
BENHAM 113
   Barzil 30, 160
   David 52, 113
   Eben 160
   Ebenezer 161
   Eli 49, 160
   John 40, 53, 104, 160
   Sarah 113
   Silas 113, 159
   Spencer 160
   Thaddeus 160
   W. R. 203
BENJAMIN 104
   Aaron 157
   Charles 266
   David 139
   Horace 207
   James 266
   John 156, 207
   Joseph 207
   Martin 156
   Orson 52–3, 105, 111
   Spencer 207
BENNELLEN
   James 162
BENNETT 42, 44, 113, 110

BENNETT (cont.)
   A. H. 66
   Abraham 107
   Alanson 70
   Amos 213
   Asa 133
   B. L. 182
   Curtis 202
   F. C. 74
   Frederick 67
   George 182
   H. 64, 133
   Ida 168
   J. 198
   James 14
   Lydia 237
   Ralph 161, 170
   Thomas 64
BENNEY
   Joseph 36
BENNIT
   Betsey 169
BENSING
   William 243
BENSON
   A. 201
   Catherine 126
   David 205, 233
   Dr. 118
   E. W. 243
   Emory 243
   George 120
   John 221
   Jonathan 232
   S. P. 255
   Seth 257
BENT 219
BENTLEY 36, 113, 227
   Betsy 215
   Edgar 233
   Isaac 233
   J. D. 232
   Samuel 230, 255
   Thomas 230, 263
   Tilness 226, 230, 232
BENTON
   C. H. 169
   Caleb 12, 16
   David 129, 148, 236
   Levi 153, 155
   Nancy 236
   Roger 33, 60
BEREZY 21
BERGE
   Elnathan 243
   Thomas 268
BERGRAN
   James 243
BERLING
   Joseph 115
BERMIE
   Alex. 129
BERNARD
   Daniel 107
   David 113
   John 182
   Timothy 37, 49
BERNER
   S. 248
BERRAY
   Azel 202
   Dinah 203
BERRENT
   E. 106

BERRY
    H. 116
    Hannah 203
    John 122, 145, 190
BERRYHILL
    Andre 108
BERRYMAN
    George 143
BESSY
    Gilbert 183
BETHUNE
    George 133
BETTS
    & Fosmire 200
    William 169
BETZ 130, f-134, 166
BIBBINS 265
BICKFORD
    A. 201
BIDDLECOME
    Daniel 203
    Otis 182
    Thomas 182
BIDLACK
    Benjamin 33, 60, 156, 169
BIGELOW 179
    Abigail 167
    Ann 167
    Charles 171
    Jefferson 183
    John 54
    Julius 256, 259
    Timothy 179, 180
BIGELOW'S RAKE FACTORY 166
BIGGINS
    James 57, 201
    Michael 201
BIGGS
    Artemus 232
BIGLOW
    Nehum 169
    Noah 60
BILINGBROKE TRACT 263
BILL
    Paul 147
    Richard 147
BILLINGHURST
    William 52
BILLINGS
    Asa 139
    B. S. 108
    Clark 266
BILLINGTON
    L. W. 232
BILLS 109
BINGHAM 17, 168
    Augustus 192
    Charles 63
BINNING
    Jeffrey 171
BIRCH
    Milan 123
BIRD
    Frederick 171
    Peter 123, 251
    William 122, 251
BIRDSALL 16
    Samuel 57
BIRDSEYE
    J. 56
    James 159, 160
BIRDSLEY
    Joseph 154
BIRNEY 91

BISHOP 132, 159, 176, 230, f-253
    Ann 115
    Asa 232
    Asher 183
    Beni 116
    Eliza 115
    Isaac 226
    James 183
    Jane 115
    John 139
    Richard 248
    Sarah 110
    Stephen 116
    William 259
BISSELL
    D. 232
    Daniel 232
    L. T. 239
    T. Jefferson 170
    William 135
BIVIN
    Joseph 253
BIXBY 259
    O. J. 171
BLACK 148
    Aaron 147
    C. E. 139
    J. 206-7
    James 130, 147-8
    John 147
    Martha 147
BLACKMAN
    Harriet 235
    Israel 161
    John 157
    Myron 235
BLACKMER 231
    Hannah 227
    Levi 19, 226-7, 231
    Joseph 14
    Myron 226
    Richmond 227
    Srah 235
BLACKMORE
    L. P. 242-3
    Lida 242
    Myron f-80
    Peter 146
BLACONS 225
BLADES
    J. H. 156
BLAIR
    Fitch & 201
    James 118
    Walter 117
BLAISDELL
    Platt 171
BLAKE
    Alexander 124
    Benjamin 258
    Hector 254
    Homer 254, 256, 258
    Ira 104
    Jane 258
    John 213, 218, 243
    Joseph 243
    Ruel 49
    Stephen 219
BLAKELY
    Jonathan 55
    Mark 120
BLAKESLEE 44
BLANCHARD
    Addison 143

BLANCHARD (cont.)
    Hiram 110
    Isaac 263
    Oscar 124
    William 108
BLECKNER
    James 157
BLINN
    Thomas 144, 171
BLISS 99
    Abraham 200
    Caleb 242
    David 183, 196
    George 96
    H. 168
    John 200, 204
    Otis 242
BLIVEN
    Benjamin 169
BLODGET 154
    A. 154
    Augustus 154
    Ephraim 154
    John 263
    Joseph 154
    Ludin 154
    Lydia 154
    Solomon 154
    Thomas 263
    William 154
BLODGETT
    Ephraim 49
BLOOD
    Harvey 168
    Israel 199, 203
    S. H. 200, 203
    Stephen 199
BLOOD'S CORNERS 253
BLOOD'S STATION 264
BLOSSOM 38, 154
    Ed 143
    W. 49, 108
    William 42, 102-4
BLOSSOM'S HOTEL 103-4
BLOUNT
    Daniel 171
    Elias 171
    Joseph 228
    Larzelier 171
    Walter 228
BLYTHE
    J.A. 168
BOARDMAN
    H. M. 156
    Jesse 155
BOCKAW
    John 123
BODDEN
    Sally 242
BODLEY
    George 171
BODMAN
    William 159-60
BODWELL
    Lewis 65
BOGART
    A. W. 104
    H. H. 69, 128
    Henry 144
    Herman 24, 69, 128-9, 133, 136
    James 53, 66, 230
    John 230
BOGERT
    H. 127

BOGERT (cont.)
James   74, 128, 135–6
John   133–4
BOHNI
John   171
BOIR
Patrick   183
BOLINGBROKE   262
BOLTON   229
BOLTWOOD
William   199
BONCHET
Alfred   124
BOND
A. G.   201
Edwin   218, 223
Hiram   201
Thomas   183, 195
BONESTEEL
P. S.   f-197, 200
Peter   201–2
Philip   201
William   183
BONNER
John   183
BONNIE
A.   127
BOOM
Stewart   213
BOON
L. L.   108
BOOTH
Caroline   188
Catherine   188
Charles   183
Cyrus   230
Danford   f-94, 188
Dolla   188
Dorris   176, 181
E. L.   243
Frederick   183
George   108, 183
H. M.   161
I. M.   113
James   205
Lucy   108
Martin   255
Ruth   176, 188
S.   60
Sally   188
Sharon   176–7, 181–2, 188, 193
Wesley   123
William   183
BOOTHE   259
BORDEN   257
Dwight   269
I. S.   257
Thomas   203
BORDWELL
Reuben   128
BORST
H.   208
BORTLE
P.   127
Peter   127, 148
BOSTONOFF
Frank   183
BOSTWICK   153
Arthur   171
Elijah   219
William   70, 74
BOSWELL
Daniel   122
F.   166

BOSWELL (cont.)
Frank   108
N. R.   182
Nathaniel   53
Schoolhouse   250
BOSWELL'S CORNERS   250
BOSWORTH
Nathan   160
BOTSFORD
Achilles   180–1
BOTTICE
James   233
BOUCK   202
William   56
BOUGHTON   24, 35, 106, 198
Abraham   18, 202
Alice   202
Asahel   198, 202, 204
Caleb   203
Claudius   52, 198, 202, 204
DeForrest   201, 202
Eleazer   199, 200–2, 204
Enos   17, 198–9
F. Augustus   207
Frederick   35, 198, 209
George   107
H.   202
Harry   202
Henry   200, 205
Hezekiah   198–9, 202
Huldah   208
J. H.   210
J. M.   210
Jared   17, 25, 30, 49, 198–200, 202, 209–10, 212
Levi   198, 200–1, 203
Lucy   202
Lyman   198
Melanie   198
Nathaniel   200, 202
Olive   198
Samuel   200, 203
Sellick   198, 202
Seymour   30, 198, 202, 212
T. M.   199
Theodosia   198
William   113, 198, 242
BOUKER
James   256
BOURN
John   139
BOURNS
Edward   75
BOUSE
Edward   158
BOWDEN   68
BOWEN   72
Jere.   241
John   257
Lydia   242
S. W.   108
BOWENS
Morris   108
BOWER
Cornelius   134
BOWERMAN
Gifford   194
James   157
BOWERS
Jacob   230
BOWKER
S.   166
BOWLES
A. G.   113

BOWMAN
Isaac   139
James   143
Thomas   143–4
BOWNE
Robert   262–3
BOYCE
Robert   104
BOYD   11, 218, 227
Benj.   232
Betsey   242
Frank   243
Ichabod   168
John   171
BOYDEN
A. L.   166
BOYES
Francis   157
BOYINGTON
Jonathan   49
BOYLE
Barney   139
BRACE
Elisha   1991 202
F. B.   199
Herman   199
Jeremiah   203
Joel   199
John   199, 202–3, 212
Norman   199
Orange   102
Reuben   199, 202
Sophia   201
T. B.   199
Thomas   204
William   199, 202
BRACKETT HOUSE   165
BRADBURY   241
BRADFORD
John   45, 132
W. H.   139
BRADLEY   166, 168
Ann   212
B.   208
Bani   212
C. W.   212
Eber   150
Frederick   221
Hannah   150
Jacob   79
Monroe   213, 223
Mortimar   213
P.   169
Samuel   63
& Smith   179
Theda   212
BRADT
Henry   121
J. Taylor   67
John   180
William   180
BRADY
Christopher   36, 181
Edward   209, 221, 224
James   183
BRAGG   91
BRAIN
William   161
BRAINARD
Daniel   17, 35, 63, 79, 101
Sears   139
BRANCH   55
Henry   256
O. A.   108

BRANDS
   William 157
BRANDT 127, 198
   Christopwer 143
   Joseph 11–3, 16, 22–3, 127
BRANSON
   Edwin 118
BRANT
   George 115
BRAUDO
   Hiram 124
BRAY
   Andrew 230
   Cyrus 150, f-151
   Harriet 150
   J. 225
   M. A. 229
BRAYTON
   I. I. 182
   James 148
BRECKENRIDGE
   John 97
BREDHOP
   William 183
BREEN
   Patrick 162
BRENNAN
   John 95
BRESHNAHAN
   Jeremiah 171
BRETT 97
BREWSTER 217
   C. G. 108
   Harriet 196
   Laura 168
   Stephen 59, 179–80
   Steven 179
   William 108
BREZEE
   John 155
BRICKLE
   Ishmael 104
BRIDGER
   Samuel 171
BRIDGES
   Henry 171
BRIDGMAN
   Alada 155
   G. D. A. 109
   George 67
   William 108, 149
BRIENDS
   William 157
BRIGGS 153, 240
   Artemus 228–30, 232, 240, 242
   Benjamin 228
   Caleb 228, 258
   Charles 266
   Cyrus 228
   Deborah 242
   Deloss 279
   Elizabeth 221
   Francis 40
   J. G. 229
   Janus 268
   Jedediah 228
   John 229, 232, 266
   Leonard 49
   Nathan 117, 233
   Nathaniel 171
   Thomas 228
   Tyler 266
   William 268
   Zack 228

BRIGGS (cont.)
   Zenus 241
BRIGHAM
   Jonas 183
BRINES
   Albert 213
BRINK
   George 213
BRISITENHAM
   Jesanina 161
BRISTOL 106
   B. I. 77
   Simeon 49
BRIZE
   Orson 130
BRIZEE 129
BROADHEAD 259
   John 15
BROCK
   Stephen 130
BROCKAWAY
   Gamaliel 146
BROCKELBANK 102, 115
   J. W. 109
   John 113, 116
   Jno. 109
   Levi 113, 116
   S. 108
   Samuel 102, 113, 116
BROCKLEBANK
   John 58
BROCKWAY
   George 169
   Harriet 169
   Polly 169
BROGAN
   James 259
BROHAW
   John 123
BRONSON 209
   Amos 209–11
   B. R. 109
   Daniel 44, 209–10, 212
   E. 49, 50, 132
   Edwin 242
   Eli 132
   F. J. 49
   Flavius 30, 208
   Lucy 211
   Philo 77, 132
   Virtue 107
BRONSONS 210
BROOK
   R. V. 243
BROOKINS
   Calvin 203
BROOKS 84
   Albert 171
   Birdseye 52
   Charles 205
   Dinah 202
   H. 116
   Hiram 204, 207
   James 217, 192
   John 123, 183
   Michael 199
   Micah 37–8, 51–2, 58, 210
   Ralph 143
BROWN 91, 119, 192, 220, 250, 258
   A. 251
   A. A. 251
   A. C. 193, 257
   Abner 191
   Allen 49, 247, 251

BROWN (cont.)
   Andrew 257
   Asa 251
   Augustus 96, 224
   Benjamin 180
   C. P. f-179, 179
   Calvin 179, 182
   Charles 143
   Cornelia 182
   Daniel 143, 231
   David 189, 191
   Dennis 255
   Edgar 171
   Edward 139
   Edwin 124
   Emily 182
   Emma 212
   Ephraim 248, 250
   F. T. 99
   Franciss 183
   Franklin 124
   George 40, 49, 232, 256
   H. 139
   H. C. 217
   H. L. f-179, 179
   H. M. 211
   H. W. 112
   Harvey 259
   Henry 142, 202, 232
   Hester 182
   Hezekiah 205
   Hiram 122, 179, 182, 251
   Ichabod 190
   J. 109, 139, 170, 265
   Jacob 45, 139
   James 52–3, 58
   Jeremiah 189, 191
   Jesse 259
   John 124, 171, 228, 230
   Joseph 163
   L. A. 190
   L. C. 243
   Levi 143
   Lincoln 168
   Maurice 258–9
   Milcah 163
   Nelson 162
   Nicholas 191
   Oliver 233
   Orland 123–4
   Orlando 257
   Otis 191
   Owen 259
   P. E. 113
   Parley 228
   Peter 104, 158, 180, 190
   R. 247
   Rachel 188
   Russel 247
   S. C. 242
   Silas 118, 220–1, 242
   Stephen 191
   Talcott 149
   Theodore 242
   Thomas 168, 182
   W. H. 139
   Walter 120
   Warren 248
   William 123, 142, 147, 168, 183, 190, 243, 256, 258
   Zurial 180, 191
BROPHY
   Thomas 139

BROSTIN
  Valentine 149
BROTHER 146
  Charles 52, 77, 146
  Henry 146
  & Hudson 105
BROTHERS
  Valentine 41, 52
BROTHERSON
  Alvin 144
BROUGH
  John 90
BROUGHTON 44
  Abraham 200
  Harry 200
BROVIE
  John 157
BROWNELL 227, 265
  George 157
  Pardon 262, 264
  Polly 117
BROWNING
  John 243
  Joseph 192
  M. J. 170
BRUCE
  Nathaniel 135
  Samuel 169
BRUGAS 33
BRUMFIELD
  James 183
BRUNDAGE 159–60
  G. F. 144
  George 154, 160
  Joseph 154
  W. H. 139
BRUNSON
  Abraham 202
  Amos 19, 88, 212
  Edward 52
  Flavius 212
  William 201
BRUSH
  M. P. 170
  W. W. 135
  William 135
BRUSHARD
  Philip 171
BRUSIE
  William 204
BRYAN
  Cornelius 183
  Prince 238, 247
  William 183
BRYANT
  Charles 183, 195
  Michael 143
  N. 53
  Prince 17
  William 108
BRYSON 242
BUCHAN 168
  Robert 159
  W. 159
  William 160
BUCHANAN
  George 122
  Jackson 121
  John 144
BUCK 35
  A. N. 180
  Addison 59, 181, 183
  D. D. 113, 132
  E. W. 264

BUCK (cont.)
  M. 180
  Moses 178
  R. 180
  Reuben 180
  Z. I. 161
  Z. J. 170
  Zina 156, 157, 203
  Ziner 113
BUCKALEW
  W. D. 135
BUCKLEY
  John 139
BUELL
  Augustus 209
  Charles 209, 211
  John 212
  Jonathan 49, 52, 53, 207
  Parker:60, 203
  T. P. 210
  Timothy 18, 44, 52, 209, 211–2
BUFORD
  John 98
BUGLES
  M. 218
BUGNEAN
  Samuel 199
BULL 91, 105
  George 108
  J. M. 161, 181
  James 121
  John 90
  Joseph 107, 108
  Richard 182
  & Stocking 104
BULLARD 120
BULLIS
  John 195
BULLOCK 257
  Barzilla 228
  George 243
  Rufus 228
  Thomas 228
BUMMONG
  Henry 142
BUMP
  Humphrey 257
  James 183
BUMPUS
  S. 201
BUNDY
  Warner 116
BUNNELL 38, 115, 180
  A. 110
  Abner 54, 118
  Abram 113
  Charles 171
  Chester 118
  Frederick 109
  H. 118
  Myron 223
  Peter 171
  Thomas 124
BUNT
  Ebenezer 147
BUONETT
  P. F. 124
BURBANK
  Jacob 232
  John 264
BURBEE 248
  Nicholas 248
BURBURT
  George 52

BURCH 105, 212
  B. H. 255
  Buel 259
  John 259, 260
  Robert 212
  Thomas 259
BURCHAM
  Henry 183
BURCHARD
  Amasa 116
  Jedediah 61
BURDEN
  James 183
BURGE
  E. W. 243
BURGER
  Chandler 116
BURGESS
  Allen 120
  Lyman 171
  Peter 120
  William 183
BURGOYNE 145
BURK
  Albert 157
BURKE
  Jacob 171
  John 183
BURKHOLDER
  Abraham 145
  John 145
  Leonard 145
BURLESON
  William 124
BURLINGG
  G. 108
BURLING PLACE 115
BURLINGAME 228
  Benjamin 218
BURLISON
  James 213
BURNETT
  James 257
  John 165
  Patrick 148, 165, 168
  William 52, 130, 166
BURNETTSON
  Edwin 195
BURNEY
  Benj. 177
  Joseph 181
BURNHAM
  Elizur 261
  H. 265
BURNS
  Harvey 143
  John 170
  Robert 183
  Timothy 49
  William 256
BURNSIDE 85, 99–100
BURR
  Aaron 14
BURRALL
  Thomas 69, 128
BURRELL
  Edward 147
  William 223
BURRIGE
  Joseph 144
BURROUGHS
  Rev. 134
BURROWS
  S. 127

BURROWS (cont.)
    Thomas 194
BURT 103
    Daniel 240
    Eben 145
    Howard 171
    J. 166, 170
    Jonathan 169, 179
    Thomass 107
    Warren 223
BURTIS 132
    C. B. 168
    Charles 168
BURTOLPH
    Milton 242
BURWELL
    Alexander 144
BUSH 208
    Andrew 160
    C. P. 159
    Charles 109
    Gilbert 193
    Henry 171
    John 161, 195
    Jonathan 161
    Rufus 213
    Samuel 159, 160
    William 208, 263
BUSH SCHOOLHOUSE 258
BUSHFIELD
    Thomas 160
BUSHNELL 218
    A. S. 228
    Asa 257
    Cleveland 263
    Jedediah 111, 203, 211, 220, 264
    & Jenks 193, 199–200
    William 199, 203–4
BUSTED
    William 67
BUTLER 95, 129, 193, 218, 248
    Chloe 119
    Daniel 121, 142
    David 256
    Eli 118, 119
    Erastus 165
    Israel 250
    J. 82, 127
    Jeremiah 148
    John 11–3, 22
    Joseph 213
    Lewis 107
    Mray 167
    Nathaniel 220
    Norman 256
    Richard 12
    Sebra 220
    W. M. 207
BUTLORON
    Jeremiah 148
BUTRICK
    Oliver 231
BUTTERFIELD 86–7
    Albert 139
    George 136
    James 144
    William 130
BUTTOLPH
    Milton 232
BUTTON
    James 254
BUTTS 226
    Luke 171
    Sylvester 124

BUZZELL
    David 265
BYRNES
    N. 212

C

CADY
    Andrew 122
    Marvin 70
    William 261–2
CAHILL
    Morris 195
CAHOON
    Allen 139
    James 258
CAIRNS
    Patrick 123
CALDWELL
    Caroline 188
    Jerusha 161
    McGee 168, 169
    Murray 180
    Olive 150
    Samuel 227
    Sophronia 203
    William 161
CALHOUN
    Robert 183
CALKINS 200
    J. G. 203
CALL
    James 267
    John 17, 33
CALLEN
    James 162
CALLISTER
    Elizabeth 161
    W. 115
    Will 161
    William 160
CALLISTER FARM 117
CALLON 117
    John 204
CALON
    R. T. 162
CALVIN
    Aldrich 192
    Isaac 192
CAMERON
    Charles 21, 31, 104, 107
    James 148, 157
    Peter 251
CAMFIELD (see Canfield)
CAMMON
    Hugh 142
CAMP
    James 213
    William 181, 183
CAMPBELL 11, 258
    Albert 163
    Arch'd 69
    Christopher 130
    Elisha 202
    James 39, 202
    Mike 144
    S. N. 112
    Ward 139
    William 168
CAMPION
    A. A. 130
CAMUS 129

CANADA
    Lyman 230
CANESQUE 261–2
CANFIELD
    Benjamin 110, 154
    Dan 218, 220
    Jason 220
    Josephh 113, 116
    Sibyl 220
    Titus 218
    William 160
CANFIELD PLACE 178
CANNON
    Hiram 200
    Jacob 257
CANOVAN
    John 171
CARDEN
    Miles 139
CAREY 66, 147, 148, 166
    Harvey 166, 170
    Isaac 171
    Lucius 18, 35, 66, 102
CARKOW
    Charles 162
CARL
    Patrick 183
CARLOUGH
    David 161
    S. J. 159
CARLTON
    Henry 258
    Thomas 113, 203
CARMAN
    George 124
    Solomon 200
    Warren 205
CARPENTER 115, 163
    Amy 113
    C. G. 168
    C. H. 166
    Calvin 171
    Charle 124
    E. G. 166
    Ichabod 234, 269
    Increase 202
    James 183, 195
    Jesse 113
    John 116–7
    Joshua 49
    Napoleaon 266
    P. 202
    R. C. 166, 168
    & Rice 166
    Samuel 113
CARPENTER BLOCK 166
CARR
    C. C. 204
    Edson 109
    Edward 157
    Edwin 49
    George 139, 148, 161
    Harrison 243, 251
    James 143
    John 139
    Owen 205
    Thomass 80, 143
    William 121, 183
CARRIER 263
    Ithaner 219, 263
CARRIGER
    William 219
CARROL
    John 142

CARROL (cont.)
  Patrick 144
  Polly 30
CARROLL
  Erastus 209
  James 204
  M. 108
  Sanford 214
  William 169
CARSON
  C. 153
  Charles 148
  Edward 161
  Jacob 183
  James 145, 183
  P. 108
  Porter 108
  Robert 145
CARTER 136
  James 63, 69, 128
  Jennie 212
  John 143
  Sackett & Fosket 118
  William 212
CARTWRIGHT
  F. 238
  Paul 124
CARY
  Thomas 157
CASE 119, 164
  Anthony 49
  B. 240, f-242
  B. A. 243
  Betsey 242
  Betty 211
  Billings 240, f-242, 243
  C. Z. 113
  Charles 220
  D. W. 231
  Daniel 117
  David 159
  E. K. 59
  Erastus 240
  Eunice 118
  George 233, 259-60
  Hiram 117, 122
  Horace 246
  James 159, 211, 239-40, 242
  John 122, 171, 240
  Joshua 159-60
  Lavina 159
  Mark 240
  Morgan 119
  Nathaniel 52
  O. 239
  Oliver 52, 53
  Orestes f-238
  S. L. 219
  Schuyler 224
  Seba 118
  Seymour 248
  William 242
  Z. T. 58
  Zadia 242
CASEY
  Henry 157
  Michael 124
CASEY'S DIV. 88-9
CASKEY
  Alva 258
  Henry 255
  Margaret 256
  Sidney 255
  W. D. 255

CASKEY (cont.)
  Willard 254, 259
CASNER
  George 259-60
CASSILTON
  Richard 124
CASSORT 159
  Charles 116
  David 115, 126
  Emily 126
  William 115
CASTELLO
  Thos. 113
CASTLE
  Charity 119
  Daniel 118
  Dyer 117-8
  Francis 112, 117
  Israel 210
  James 118
  L. B. 170
  Lemuel 117, 119
  Levi 156
  Oliver 121
  S. G. 210
CASWELL
  Asa 176
CATHCART 200
CATLIN
  John 154
  Lucy 154
  Lyman 170
  Oren 148
CATON
  George 161-2
  Henry 161
  John 34, 168
  Reuben 163
  Thomas 171
CATTERSON
  John 139
CAVANAGH
  Michael 221
CAYTON
  Robert 142
CAYWARD
  John 156
CERRIGAN
  Daniel 234
CHABERS (see Chambers)
CHADWICK
  J. 61
  Jabez 265
CHAFFEE
  Henry 265
CHAMBERLAIN 55, 108, 119
  F. O. 104, 118
  Frank 108, f-114
  Frederick 223
  Hortentius 122
  I. 259
  J. 258
  James 104, 183
  John 136
  M. 255
  O. W. 121, 124
  Phebe 231
  Pierce 19, 227
  R. G. 121
  R. S. 124
CHAMBERLAYNE
  Israel 169
CHAMBERLIN
  I. 257

CHAMBERLIN (cont.)
  John 257
  William 256, 258-9
CHAMBERS 259
  Horace 218
  John 128
  Joseph 218
  William 222
CHAMPION
  J. P. 166
  Thornton 171
CHAMPLAIN
  John 157
  Lewis 157
  Samuel 10
CHANDLER
  George 232
  Samuel 201
  William 157
CHANNING 47
  Henry 112
  Thomas 105
CHAPIN 22, 26, 44, 107, 210, 219, 160, 264
  Abigail 112
  Asa 259
  Betsey 65
  Charles 114, 161
  Dan 52
  Daniel 207-8, 211-2
  Erastus 223
  George 53, 159
  H. 29, 56
  Heman 207
  Henry 108, 110
  Herman 49, 52
  I. 107
  Israel 13, 16-9, 22-3, 29, 32, 35, 40, 52, 56, 78-9, 101, 103, 112, 114, 160, 261
  James 161
  John 63, 65
  Lewis 211
  O. C. 207, 210
  Oliver 207
  Ralph 53
  Robert 53, 59
  Sallie 29
  Seth 130
  Silas 130
  Spencer 107
  Stephen 171
  T. 107-8
  Thaddeus 29, 32, 37, 44-5, 49, 52, 58, 66, 79, 80, 102-3, 106, 110, 112
  William 162
CHAPIN'S MILL 114
CHAPLIN
  Jonathan 256
CHAPMAN 61, 79, 132, 168, 219, 257
  Aaron 243
  Amasa 126
  Amos 259
  Benjamin 18, 209, 211
  Betsey 242
  Charles 161
  Dennis 160
  Emily 126
  Ezekiel 241
  J. 61, 156
  Jedediah 61, 69, 129, 132, 148, 160, 169
  John 132, 167, 211, 242
  Lewis 159-60
  Mary 150
  Rebecca 159
  Robert 243

CHAPMAN (cont.)
Sallie 242
Samuel 213
Thomas 116
William 183
CHAPPEL
Edgcomb 49
CHAPPMAN
Jedediah 34
CHARLTON 145
CHASE, 67, 126, 168
Abner 156, 169
Amos 265
D. S. 161
G. H. 131
H. A. 131
Homer 50, 116
Howard 183
J. E. 126
Jacob 136, 242
James f-125
Julia 126
L. D. 161
Philander 34, 102, 110-1
R. G. 131
R. G. & Co. 50
Walter 164
CHATFIELD
Curtis 154
Jesse 256
Oliver 154
CHAUMONOT
Father 33, 197
CHEESEBORO
N. G. 38, 43, 107, 111, 254
CHENEY
Altie 226
Charless 82
Darwin 53
E. W. 111, 226
George 80
CHESEBRO
Betsey 254
Caroline 254
Charles 108-9
E. C. 109
Edmund 80
H. O. 64, 66, 254
Henry 51
Nicholas 64
CHESLEY
J. 127
CHESTER
Charles 182
Thomas 132
CHEW
A. L. 58
CHILD
J. 52
CHILDS
A. S. 159
Austin 160
Caleb 24
E. A. 160
Homer 148
Jonathan 209
Joseph 24, 146
Phoebe 24
Theron 149
CHILSON
Cassius 195
Emer 255
William 195
CHIPMAN 116, 230-1

CHIPMAN (cont.)
Altie 226
Cyrus 19, 226-7, 230-1
Edward 81
H. D. 109
L. 232
Lemuel 19, 51-2, 58, 79, 226-7, 230-2
Lina 231
Nathaniel 232
Reese 211
Rev. 118
Samuel 37, 226, 231
T. 231
W. M. 108
W. Mynderse 112
CHISSOM
Samuel 57
CHRISLER
S. D. 139
CHRISTIAN
Abbott 119
Ashbury 110, 115
G. A. 116
CHRISTIE
Duncan 257
CHRISTY
Andrew 266
CHRONABERRY
Frank 183
CHRYSLER
Nicholas 180
CHUBBUCK
James 157
CHURCH 102
A. M. 108
Ambrose 106, 108
Charles 172
E. C. 108
John 160
Philip 39
Richard 80
W. C. 180
W. S. 129
CHURCH'S TAVERN 104
CHURCHILL 44
CLAFFIN
E. M. 214
Jeremiah 213
CLAPP
Alfred 90, 171, 183
Charles 171
D. E. 93
Dexter 170, 171
Henry 132
Sarah 82-a
CLARE
William 257
CLARK 41, 72, 147, 166, 227, 235, 250, 258-9, 265
Albert 268
Bartlett 255, 258
Benjamin 18, 35, 262
C. R. 220
Caleb 103
Charless 123
Cornelius 171
D. Laurence 134
E. A. 167
Edward 269
Elijah 230, 263-4
Francis 182
G. 219
Gains 130
Galgutha 124

CLARK (cont.)
George 107, 220, 234
Godfrey 232
Grace f-253
Henry 53
Hovey 108
Isaac 171
J. 56, 127
James 111, 168
Joel 117, 202
Jno. 29
John 17, 34, 49, 54, 63, 70, 103-4, 107, 111, 117, 124
Joseph 49, 117, 262-4
Laura 152
Lorenzo 37, 52, 263
Lovina 263
Lucy 263
Lydia 263
Lyman 53
M. H. & Co. 105
Mary 264
Myron 51, 53, 105, 263-4
Nathan 263
Noah 50, 112
Orra 232
Orrin 34, 69-71, 73, 111
Orris 135
Polly 264
Ralph 131
Rebecca 263
S. 180
Samuel 144
Shubeal 159
& Stanley 104
Submit 263
T. 169
Thena 263
Thomas 124
W. W. 121
Walter 157
Warren 262, 265
William 18, 49, 88, 142-3, 162, 261, 263, 266
Wyllis 63
CLARKE 88
E. C. 81
John 234
Lewis 122
N. T. 78
Noah 112-3
William 53, 117
CLARY 163
CLAYTON
J. K. B. 156
James 142
CLEAR
John 183
Tim 144
CLEAR SKY 23
CLEMENS 145
CLEMENT
Hamlet 243
Henry 124
CLEVELAND 104, 107, 159, 265
A. 108
E. 49, 53, 265
Eph. 37
Ephraimm 40, 52, 261-2, 264
M. H. 261
M. M. 108
Martha 264
Olive 263
S. C. 67

CLEVELAND (cont.)
Susan 263
W. 37, 264
CLEVELAND PLACE 208
CLIMMONS
Catharine 169
CLINE
John 200
W. H. 203
William 124, 214
CLINTON 219
Dewitt 39, 56, 78, 130, 180
George 12, 26, 32-3, 53, 78, 114
James 11, 14
Margaret 192
CLOFLIN
George 218
CLOHEY
John 121
CLOHESY
Edward 121
CLOWEES
Timothy 45
CLOY
Sarah 167
CLOYES
Benjamin 183
CLYNE
Peter 191
COAL
George 143
COAN
Elisha 201-2
COATES
Calvin 181
Irving 182
J. 181
James 177
Joshua 181
COATS
C. 170
C. S. 132
Calvin 156, 170
Charles 162
Cuyler 171
William 178
COBB
Charles 172
Collins 205
Cullen 172
E. S. 65, 108
Job 232
Stewart 129
COBERLY
Joseph 163
COBURN
Asher 242
Ebenezer 231
Esther 242
John 139
COCHLOF
Charles 243
COCHRANE
John 104, 232
CODDING 18, 40, 209, 225
Abigail 211
Burt 18, 239, 240
Faunce 239, 241, 242
George 18, 35, 25, 40, 49, 114, 211, 225, 239-42
Henry 243
John 18, 78, 225, 239, 241
Luscomb 242
Polly 242

CODDING (cont.)
Robert 239
S. A. 40
Sarah 209, 241
Stephen 239, 242
William 18, 40, 243
CODDINGTON 57
COE 38
B. D. 55
Belah 103
C. H. 55
Chauncey 55, 108
John 64, 167
Samuel 16
COE'S HOTEL 56
COE'S STAGEHOUSE 55
COFFIN 155
Jared 12
COFFY
William 142
COGSWELL
William 40
COGWARDS 156
COHEACY
J. B. 108
COLBERT
James 54
Lloyd 54
COLBRAITH
William 12
COLBURN
James 171
Jonathan 242
Joshua 232
Lucy 242
COLBY
Enoch 229, 230
COLE
Abner 69, 128
C. H. 84
Charles 172
Daniel 266
Elmer 265
George 142
Heman 259
Henry 28
Hezekiah 256
Ira 139
J. 166
James 64, 170, 259
John 256
L. W. 109
Luther 17, 55, 79, 102
Nathaniel 53
Reuben 256
Southwick 153-4
Spencer 211
COLEGMORE
Willet 157
COLEGROVE
Hiram 258
Jairus 257
COLEMAN 68, 91, 132
Chester 64
E. R. f-107
Eliphalet 79, 160
George 139
Mary 147
Michael 143
Richard 157
Thomas 40
W. H. 133
COLF
Benjamin 183

COLGROVE 258
Hiram 49, 253, 254
Peter 113
COLL
Thomas 157
COLLAN
Bill 30
COLLAR
Chester 145
COLLIDGE
Emma 166
COLLIER 134
Joseph 134
COLLINS 180, 227
A. 217
A. C. 204
Aaron 209, 211, 232, 242, 251
Ann 126
Cyprian 18, 207
Edward 124
Francis 143
Frederick 210
G. 217
Isaac 104
J. 127
James 116
John 49, 124, 135-6, 157
M. N. 108
Peter 183
S. 251
Tyrannus 207
COLLISTER
C. J. 207
Robert 257, 259
COLYER
Stephen 199
COLMEY
J. 200
COLQUHOUN
Patrick 20-1, 31, 127
COLT
J. 127
Joseph 21, 34, 59, 111, 136
Judah 17, 21, 25, 39, 53, 63, 78-9, 101, 115
S. 127
Samuel 24, 64, 69, 73, 128-9, 135-6
COLTON
Andrew 202
COLVIN
Isac 204
Michael 205
COLWELL 145
Deborah 169
William 145
COMBS
& Cross 106
Jonathan 183
Samuel 171
COMFORD
William 172
COMPSON 98-9
H. B. 99
COMPTON
Sophronia 196
COMSTOCK 24, 54, 113, 190, 195
Augustus 191
D. 56
Darius 17, 49, 189, 192, 194
Harlow 112
Jared 192-3
John 192
Joseph 192
N. 194

COMSTOCK (cont.)
    Nathan 17, 18, 41, 59, 114, 189, 191–2, 194
    Otis 17, 35, 189–3
    Truman 157
    Zeno 191
CONDE 55
CONDON
    Andrew 124
    William 123
CONE 206, 208, 219
    A. 207
    Andrew 211
    Edna 159
    James 159
    Linus 212
    Noah 219
CONEY
    William 224
CONGDEN 57
CONGDON
    James 162
CONGER 129
    M. 132
    N. W. 124
CONKLIN
    Abram 258
    Benjamin 258
    Edward 108
    Luther 211
    Robert 144, 172
    Thomas 144, 171
    Vincent 230
CONLEY
    Michael 163
CONN 167
CONNEL
    Ichabod 266
CONNELLY 67
CONNERS
    Joseph 162
CONNOLLY
    James 162
CONNORS
    George 162
CONOVER
    Cornelius 200
    William 198–9
CONRAD
    Geo. 147
    William 147
CONROY
    Daniel 183
    James 162
CONVERSE
    John 171
CONVEY
    Patrick 143
CONWAY
    John 156
    Owen 156
    Thomas 157
COOK 58
    Abram f-172, 183
    C. A. 77
    Charles 58, 130
    Daniel 130
    David 64, 69, 128–30, 136
    Ebenezer 169
    G. B. 155
    George 52, 59, 65–6, 106
    H. 108
    Heman 230
    Isaac 163

COOK (cont.)
    James 203
    Jonathan 157
    Mahala f-172
    Marcus 143
    Mary 163
    Pamelia 163
    R. D. 58
    Richard 170
    Robert 65, 104
    Sheldon 171, 183
    & Thompson 155
    Trueworthy 14
    Walter 161
    & Waters 192
    Z. 136
COOKE 135
    Samuel 135
COOL 168
COOLEY 105, 115, 166
    A. B. 50
    A. D. 166
    Adalinee 126
    Albert 117
    Ann 126
    Aug. 108
    Catherine f-122, 126
    Eliza 169
    Emily 126
    Francis 126
    Frederick 117, 126
    Hannah 119
    Hiram 126
    J. S. 105
    James 49, 105
    John 40, 117, 122, 126
    Justin 169
    Justus, Jr. 183
    Lucian 126
    Luciana 126
    Lucina 126
    Lydia 126
    Lyman 126, 183
    Margaret 126
    Martha 126
    May 126
    Minerva 126
    N. N. 105
    Nathaniel 114
    Nellie 126
    Orin 126
    Reny 169
    S. & Co. 105
    Terrissa 126
COOLIDGE
    C. C. 166
COOLIES (Cooley's) 147
COON
    Aaron 213
    J. L. 139
    John 166
    T. H. 139
    Valentine 179
COONER
    William W. 124
COONEY
    Lawrence 139
    Lorentus 268
COONS
    R. N. 264
COOPER
    A. V. 68
    Albert 205
    Allen 124

COOPER (cont.)
    Almon 205
    Anson 205
    Charles 144
    Edward 139
    John 52, 217
    Lester 183
    Otowell 213
    Samuel 190
    Simeon 183
    William 223
    Willis 224
COOPER'S BLACKSMITH SHOP 167
COPP
    E. D. 182
    E. Darwin 172
COPELAND
    John 113, 155, 221
CORBIN
    E. S. 131, 182
    Edward 64
CORCORAN
    Richard 124
    Walter 57
COREY
    Andrew 123
CORLEAR 10
CORLISS 220
CORNELL 134
    Amaziah 263
    George 90
    John 233
    M. E. 90
    Merwyn E. 243
    Robert 124
    Stephen 90
CORNING 83–5
    Erastus 86
CORNISH
    Amaziah 262
CORNPLANTER 12, 15, 22–4
CORNWALL
    William 52
CORP
    George 144
CORS
    George 172
CORSON
    Derrick 160
    J. 108
    Jacob 105
CORTELSON
    William 130
CORWIN
    R. Francis 171
    Samuel 170
CORY
    Albert 268
COSINE
    Joseph 143
COST
    Elias 45, 49, 52, 169
    Elizabeth 159
    Farm 116
    Jacob 181
    Jesse 52, 181
    John 159, 181
COSTELLO
    John 256
    Thomas 254, 258
COSTON
    Michael 158
COTTON
    Edward 196

COUCH 84
    D. 116
COUGHLIN
    Michael 142
COUNMUS
    James 124
COUNTRYMAN
    J. F. 136
COURSEN
    Derrick 159
COURSEY 129
    Thomas 130
COURTNEY
    Edward 124
    Patrick 122, 161
COVEL 248
    Eben 265
    James 248, 262, 264
    Thomas 248, 251
COVER
    John 193
COVERT
    Nelson 53
COVILL 232
    Abijah 202
    D. L. 53
    H. H. 202
COVILLE
    Aldin 199
COWAN'S BATTERY 85
COWARD
    George 49
COWDERY
    Oliver 42-3
COWDRY
    Frank 67
COWING 218
COWLEY
    Isaac 143
COX
    William 178
COXE 75, 203
    Arthur 76, 182
COY
    Charles 108
    Isaiah 124
    Joseph 120
COYE
    David 249, 251
    H. D. 249
    Luke 249
COYKENDALL
    Arnold 259
    C. A. 256
    Coe 258
    Dwight 259-60
    E. 259
    Harvey 259
    J. 259
    Jerry 259
    Joel 257, 259
    Jonathan 259
    Joseph 259-60
    Jotham 258
    M. 256
    Thomas 254
    W. 256
    Zelotus 258
COYLE
    C. & T. 105
    M 108
CRAFT 153, 155
    James 67

CRAIG
    Lyman 182
CRAIN 100
    Byron 99, 183
    Henry 183
    William 183
CRAM
    Jacob 211, 231
CRAMER
    John 195
CRANDALL 192
    Amos 53
    C. L. 207
    Charles 121, 168, 267
    H. N. 218, 219
    Horatio 217
    John 241
    Margaret 242
    Phoebe 242
    Sheridan 222
    V. P. 179
CRANE 119, 166
    Aaron 104
    Abigail f-253
    Benjamin 257
    Calvin 249
    Charles 53
    Clara 181
    E. F. 119
    Elam 34, 102, 120, 160, 190, 249, f-253
    Ellen 113
    Ezekiel 159
    George 120, 249, f-250, f-253
    Joel 113
    John 102, 180, 249, f-253
    Lyman 182
    O. N. 109, 148
    Oscar 108
    O. W. 109
    P. 131
CRANE
    Sarah f-253
CRANK
    T. W. 203
CRANSTON 164
CRARY
    B. 166
CRATSLEY
    F. 257
    Jacob 256
    Joseph 256
CRAVEN
    Andrew 139
CRAWFORD
    Charles 139
    David 232
    Davis 227
    Jno. 124
    Robert 230
    Thomas 38
    Ziba 167
CREED
    James 157
    Jonathan 156
CREGAN
    John 163
CRIPPEN
    Ralph 267
CRITES
    Ebenezer 218
CRITTENDEN 168
    Albert 53
    Benjamin 162
    Canadice 155

CRITTENDEN (cont.)
    Fannie 168
    O. E. 117
    Orin 155
    Osse 164
    Sabra 155
    W. W. 148
    Warner 147
    Warren 168
    William 168
CROCKER
    Andrew 180
    George 195
    Jonathan 120
    S. P. 64
    Stephen B. 204
CROFUT
    Jonathan 120
CRONK
    John 264
    Joseph 263
CROOK
    General 97
CROOKER
    Franklin 49, 250
    Thomas 211
CROOKS f-80, 100, 236
    David f-80, 225-6, 229, 231
    Dr. 225, 231
    Eli 226, 230
    Eunice 226
    Franklin f-253
    Heman 225-6
    J. C. K. 226
    Polly 226
    Rachel 226
    Riley 226, 230
    Samuel 98, 228
    Sanford 225-6
    Sarah 226
    William 225-6
    Zada 226
CROSBY 67
    A. D. 166
    Alpheus 183
    Augustus 172
    Cornelius 167
    H. 166
    Horton 171
    John 183
    Prescott 166
    Reuben 222
    Samuel 242
    Theodore 49
    Timothy 17
    W. F. 167
    W. L. 124
    William 166, 171
CROSHIER (See Croshier)
    O. L. 110
CROSS 106
    J. C. 110
    James 110
    Joseph 170
    Russell 157
    Samuel 259
CROSSEN
    Lewis 259-60
CROSSMAN
    John 219
CROUCH
    Betsy 248
    Daniel 168
    S. 247, 249

CROW
Erastus 49
John 240
CROWELL 218
Benjamin 218
Silas 221
CROWIN
Daniel 212
CROWLEY
John 105
Michael 162
CROZIER
A. 57
CRUM 117
CRUTHERS 145
CUDDBECK
Nelson 183
CULBERTSON
John 228
CULVER 146
Cales 148
George 259
John 202
Jonathan 201
Oliver 49, 52
Robert 49
William 227
CUMMINGS
Alonzo 123
E. M. 34
Frank 213
Joanna 30
Joseph 266
Lyman 53, 265
Orlando 261
T. 210
Thomas 123
CUNNINGHAM
Dennis 183
John 144
CURRAN
Francis 124
John 160
CURRIER
George 183
James 120
Josiah f-253
CURTIS 119, 167, 217, 232
Allen 214
Barbara 168
C. C. 228
Charity 169
Daniel 217, 220
Ebenezer 18, 212, 216–7, 220
Eugene 96
George 112, 183
Hannah 220
John 40
Julius 212, 217
Lemuel 232
Margaret 168
Rhoda 220
Sylvester 227
William 116
CURTISS 105
Ebenezer 40
Julius 202
Waldo 53, 264
CUSH
William 183
CUSTER 98–9
G. A. 99
CUTBUSH
Edward 75

CUTLER 98
John 83, 120
CUTTING
John 201
CUYLER
Abraham 12
George 179
R. 127
Richard 21

D

DAGGET
Jacob 263
Oliver 112
DAIL
Francis 162
DAILY
Michael 121
William 190
DAKIN
E. 131
DALE
Christopher 162
DALLINGHAM
Thomas 123
DALLON
Michael 161
DALRYMPLE
Asa 258
DALTON
Michael 172
DALY
Charles 183
DAMOND
John 143
DANFORTH 25
Asa 14, 30
DANIEL 169
DANIELS
Albert 102, 233, 251
Daniel 219
J. 225
William 219
DANTON
John 264
William 219
DANZINGER
I. &. Co. 104
DARBEY
Morgan 143
DARLING
Alden 169
Ely 257
H. P. 160
Hannah 169
Jabez 258
John 255
Samuel 257
DARROW 30, 146
Charles 142
Hiram 57, 146
Washington 146
DATE
William 157
DATRO
James 156
DAVANPORT
Andrew 222
Norman 222
DAVIDS
R. 228
Uriah 263

DAVIDSON 84
J. 257
Robert 159
DAVIDSON'S BRIGADE 83–4
DAVINNEY
Joseph 130
DAVIS 129, 153, 228, 259
Benjamin 98, 123
Bethuel 257
C. H. 264
C. G. 250
Clarissa 65
Daniel 107
David 120
& Dewey 105
E. S. 64
Eugene 144
Ezra 255
Floyd 139
Frank 213, 243
H. M. 115
Henry 110, 224
Ira 221
Isaac 102, 111, 144
J W. 248
James 212
Jared 251
Jno 124
John 143, 157
Jonah 60
Justus 258
L. O. 259
Lora 202
Luke 168
Seth 70, 211
Sylvester 44, 177–8
Thomas 160
Uriah 88
W. W. 249
Wesley 120
William 132
DAVY
Samuel 161
Squire 60
DAWBY
Philander 167
DAWLEY 53
DAWSON
Mark 183
DAY 258
Benjamin 58, 108
Daniel 163
David 66
Henry 108
Hiram 107
J. H. 156
Liberty 16, 115
S. M. 242
S. Mills 232
Samuel 18, 114, 154
Warren 155, 232, 242
DAYKIN
E. 230
DAYTON
Abraham 15, 25
D. D. 132
David 161
DEAN 14, 18, 155, 263
Charles 157
Joel 123
Lucius 192
M. 140
Sally 35
Samuel 268

DEAN (cont.)
Seth 18, 114, 164–5
W. W. 203
Walter 130
DEANE
James 12, 14
DEARBORN
Frederick 162
DEBARTSCH 32
DEBARTZEH
Dominique 12–3
DE BOW 115
Ansel 115
DE CASSON 33
DECKER
Benjamin 172
Isaac 172
Luman 172
Martin 205
Oliver 172
Vincent 234
William 123, 254
DEDRICH
Lyman 251
DEDRICK
Lyman 265
DEETS
George 195
DEFAUT
Henry 121
DEGALINEE 33
DEGO
S. S. 68
DE GRAFF 154
Clarissa 150
Jno. 157
John 148–50, f-150
Susannah 150
DE LA BARRE 10
DELAMATER
Henry 144
DE LANCEY 75, 111, 130, 132
William 132, 135, 169
DELANO & GREEN 119
DE LARME
J. 161
DE LA SALLE
Robert 35
DE LIANCOURT 255, 191
DELIVAN
John 161
DE LORM
Joseph 182
DE LOS LLOYD
Eugene 223
DELURY
Owen 142
DEMERITT
Charles 122
DEMERRITT
John 121
DE MILL
Isaac 228
DEMING
J. P. H. 179
Simeon 210
W. 210
DEMPSEY
Jeremiah 123
John 124
DENGER
Arthus 149
DENNETT
D. 127

DENNING
John 123
DENNIS
Alexander 144, 172
Elias 191
Franklin 143
Jacob 144
James 203
John 120, 124, 132, 172
DENNIS 115
DENNISON
Asa 19, 226–7, 231, 256
Cynthia 227
Daniel 162, 183
Harriet Mead 227
Hiram 183
John 130, 140
Wm. 130
Zebediah 227
DENNIZ
Henry 140
DE NONVILLE 9–11
DE NOUVILLE 197–8, 206
DENSMORE 242
E. 53
G. W. 60
James 162
K. 179
Thomas 146
Vimri 159
Warren 162
Zora 145
Zorah 168
DENTON
Henry 124
Le Roy 122
N. N. 123
P. 264
R. 68
DE PEN
Abijah 172
Henry 180
Hiram 159
Lucy 159
N. A. 156
DE PUE 208
DEPUE
Henry 161
J. 159
John 161
Moses 159
Thomas 234
William 161
DERAMSEY
Patrick 140
DEREGGE
H. 212
DERR 159
DE SMIDT
Marenus 223
DE ST CROIX
Louis 144
DETMAR
Ignatius 140
DETRO
Charles 157
DETTER
William 162
DEVEY
Wilila 242
DEVINE
James 180
DEVLIN
Timothy 169

DEW
Erasmus 172
DEWEY
A. L. 53
Albert 53
Anna 177
Bernard f-58
& Davis 105
E. B. 55, 182
Edmund 49, 162
Elam 181
Ellen f-58
Eugene f-58
Gertrude f-58
Henry 183
Ida f-58
J. 257
Jedediah 52–3, 176, 177
Lanson 52, f-58
Mary Ann f-58
Rowland 176
Thomas f-58
DE WITT
H. C. 168
M. H. 263
William 154
DEXTER
J. E. 77
DEY
David 144
Francis 130
Frank 144
Henry 130
DEY
W. S. 136
Warren 258
DEYO
A. L. G. 268
Ellery 269
Ira 265, 266
DEYS
C. W. 108
DE ZENG 129
Edward 169
F. A. 69
Fred 128
Frederick 69
W. S. 129
Wililam 72, 129, 136
DIBBLE 32
Cassius 211
Eliza 212
George 213
Horace 207, 212
Joseph 207
Pratt 183
Spencer 212
DICKENSON
Orman 267
DICKERSON
F. D. 155
I. 120
DICKINSON
A. P. 100
Augustus 40, 165, 168
Charles 172, 222
Cotton 35
Daniel 198
DeEstain 97
Elias 164
Henry 205
M. O. 202
N. O. 198–200
S. B. 212

DICKINSON (cont.)
  W. D. 198
  William 49
DICKSON
  Hubbard 195
  John 37, 52, 217
DIEDRICH
  Peter 146
DILLEN
  William 68, 115
DILLENBECK
  A. J. 146
  Charles 144
DILLINGHAM
  F. 200
  Jephtha 191
  & Stotenberg 166
DILLON 166
  Hiram 160
  John 190
  William 121, 198, 196
DIMMOCK
  Lydia 168
DIMOCK
  Solomon 168
DINGLEY
  B. R. 108
DINGMAN
  Lavant 143
DITROW
  Michael 143
DIVNINER
  William 140
DIX
  Morgan 75
DIXON
  A. 218
  Amos 228, 257
  Andrew 160
  Benjamin 148
  E. S. 147
  J. G. 146
  James 235
  John 30, 143, 146–7, 215, 228
  Mary 215
  Milton 269
  S. W. 219
  W. J. 217
DOAN
  William 124
DOANE 136
  Ann 135
  George 135
  Jona. 128
  Jonathan 69, 128, 135
  Mary 135
DOBBIN
  Hugh 136
DOBBINS 45, 201
DOBSON 265
DODD 167
DODDINGTON
  Mark 143–4
DODGE 264
  Anson 145
  Elizbeth 30
  Frank 148
  Rebecca 119
DOLAN
  Thomas 172
DOLSON 31
DONALDSON 258
DONGAN 10

DONIELSON
  Isaac 243
DONNELLY 82, 83
  Dudley 82
  George 140
DONOGH
  J. W. 169
DONOLDS
  Joseph 166
DOOLITTLE 258
  A. W. 258
  Asa 208
  H. H. 172
  Henry 258
  Jefferson 259
  John 78, 205
  Mark 119
  Orlin 169
  Polly 152
  Stillman 119
  T. 259
  Thomas 258, 259
  Willard 233
  William 258
DORAN
  Richard 172
DORCHESTER 58
  Charles 144
  James 130
DORE
  George 222
  John 139
DORMAN
  A. 147
  J. S. 147
  Joel 49
  Mr. 147
DORRANCE
  John 183
  Samuel 178
DORRENCE
  Ellen 242
  May 242
  Roxana 242
  Thomas 242
DORRINGTON 38
DORSEY
  Daniel 52, 54, 170
  John 183
  Walter 183
DOTEY 102
DOTY
  Chester 211
  E. 180
  Elisha 116
  Ellis 110–1, 130
  George 243
  Gilbert 234
  William 241
DOUBLEDAY
  Jerome 183
DOUD
  John 207
DOGHERTY
  John 183
DOUGLAS 58, 81–2
  Alexander 149
  Andrew 172
  Lewis 172
  S. 115
  S. J. 265
  Sarah Ann 178
  Stephen 39, 81, 178
  William 75

DOUGLASS
  Henry 155
  William 113
DOW
  Lorenzo 60
DOWD
  Jno. 211
DOWDIN 208
DOWNER
  Jacob 183
DOWNING
  Benjamin 230
DOWNS 217
  Edmond 229
  Elizabeth 220
  Griffing 220
  John 183
DOWNY
  Thomas 142
DOX 129, 136
  A. 69, 128
  Abraham 52, 69, 128, 136, 230
  G. 128
  G. L. 128
  Gerritt 130
  J. 69
  Jacob 130
  John 52–3, 130
  Myndert 128
  Peter 52, 133
  Stephenn 143–4
  Theodore 143
DOYLE 227
  Aaron 243
  Samuel 123
DRAIFN
  Henry 143
DRAKE 83
  A. H. 144
  Charles 268
  Edward 268
DRAPER
  A. P. 168
  Daniel 256
  G. 60
  Gideon 60
  James 53
  John 59, 105
  Phili 180
  Stephen 259
DRENNAN
  Karina 140
DRISCOL
  Timothy 213
DRISCOLL
  T. 207
DROHAN
  Edward 266
DROWNE
  Samuel 200
DROYER
  Patrick 140
DRUM
  Francis 143
  Lewis 143
DRUMMER
  John 124
DRUMMOND 44
DRURY
  J. 127
  L. M. 52
  Leander 104
  Parley 228
DRYER 199

DRYER (cont.)
C. B. 168
Caroline 202
G. H. 232
George 199
M. C. 203
Rufus 199, 202, 204
Samuel 201
Thomas 109
Truman 197–9, 203
W. C. 198, 204
William 52, 197–9, 202
W. S. 68, 166
DUBOE
Albert 169
DUBOIS
Anson 134
J. F 115
DUCKINFIELD
Edwin 143
DUDLEY 28, 29, 102–3
Abraham 208
Martin 17, 101
S. B. 208
Sally 28
Tavern 103
DUEL
Timothy 212
DUELLE
Roderick 183
DUER
William 72
DUFF
D. A. 133
DUFFIN
Patrick 163
DULY
John 157
DUNBAR 147
Mary 65
DUNCAN 102, 110, 221
A. 49
Alexander 80, 111
William 80
DUNGAn
Samuel 32, 102
DUNHAM
Carter 243
Dvid 33, 60
Mark 267
Timothy 160
DUNKLE
Charles 172
George 161
Lewis 172
DUNLAP 15
James 121
DUNMORE
Irena 242
DUNN
A. 168
Alexander 40
Emmett 142
James 213
Owen 183
Patrick 172
Thomas 139
Timothy 158
William 250
DUNNIGAN
Hugh 144, 157
John 143
Michael 110
DUNNING 130

DUNNING (cont.)
Henry 233
William f-92,130
DURAND 114, 118
B. 118
Elias 125
Henry 119
DURBIT
William 109
DURFEE
Elizabeth 189
Stephen 30
DURFUR
Leonard 142
DURGAN
Daniel 53
DURGY
Ira 110, 259
DURHAM 50
John 172
DURKEE
Daniel 184
George 140, 184
DURMAN
Jacob 158
DURPEE
Manley 142
DURRANT
W. P. 130
William 64
DUSENBERRE 77
George 52, 77, 78
DUSENBERRY 240
Lucy 246
W. H. 246
DUSINBERRE
G. B. 54
W. B. 58
DUTTON 146–7
C. H. 243
William 89
DUVALLE
Abner 153
DUVILL
Charles 157
DWELLE
Delafield 157
DWIGHT 34, 77
A. L. 108
Francis 34, 67, 77
H. 69
Henry 57–8, 129
DWYER
John 108
DYER
Jacob 63

E

EADS 192
EGAN
Anthony 205
EAGER
James 124
EARL
Jesse 136
Solomon 17
EARLE
John 201, 218
EARLY 98–9
Army 97
J. A. 212
James 212

EASTER
John 113
EASTMAN
Abel 257
Hiram 53
James 172
John 214
William 172
EASTO
Charles 143
Henry 143
EATON 66, 116, 119, 208
Cyral 120
Eben 66
Farm 120
Henry 144
Nancy 256
Timothy 156
EBERT
Frederick 157
Michael 195
ECKLEY
George 145
EDDINGTON
W. F. 130
EDDY 38
Ansel 112, 155
George 184
Jacob 180
Moses 180
EDGAR
A. D. 156
EDGARTON
Washington 124
EDGERTON
Volney 52, f-62
W. Irving 172
EDGETT
John 256
EDIE
James 66
EDINGTON
Philip 146
W. F. 146
EDMANSON
Thomas 160
EDMONSTEN
Owen 53
EDMONSTON
J. 166
Thomas 182
EDMUNSTON
Owen 169
Thomas 169
EDSON
E. 156
J. L. 156
J. 212
William 169, 182
EDWARDS
Benjamin 172
Charles 160, 172
John 123, 172
Jonathan 40, 114
S. 218
EGGLESTON
Elisha 217, 219
Henry 144, 172
Jesse 144, 172
Josiah 217
EGGLESTON 208
Moses 208
Nathaniel 216–7
Silas 208, 212

EGGLESTONE
Silas 230
EHRLICH
T. A. 105
EIGHMEY
Amos 172
Charles 121
James 121
William 172
ELDRIDGE
Amos 204
Barber 267
Clark 117
Ezekial 160
John 224
Thomas 256
ELLAS
A. D. L. f-158
ELLIOT
Casina 184
Nathan 79
ELLIOTT 19
Andrew 20
Benjamin 20
Henry 153
Joseph:20, 32
ELLIS 82, 96, 128, 202, 218
Albion 80, 112
B. 53, 201
Boliver 53, 64, 204
Charles 124, 254, 256, 258
Charlotte 258
D. 201
Elijah 154, 159
George 144
Marvel 262
& Parmalee 105
S. W. 108
Stephen 202
Vilate 201
William 82, 108
ELLSWORTH
Dyer 144, 172
ELLSWORTH 86
John 142
ELLWANGER
Federick 205
ELMORE 113
ELWELL
Hannah 152
ELY
Ebenezer 107
Herman 79
Isaac 232
EMBRY
Thomas 193, 199–200
EMBURY
Edmond 211
EMERSON
Austin 124
B. K. 115
EMERY
Charles 124
EMMONS 208
Alexander 18, 207
Daniel 208
E. 207
Oliver 207
Richmond 243
William 218
EMORY 96
ENGEL
William 154

ENNIS
Abraham 155
Robert 204
ENSIGN
Harry 196
Henry 251
James 251
ENTRICKEn
William 180
ERDLE
Jacob 217
ERMIS
Isaac 224
ESTES
James 196
ESTY 159
A. B. 145
William 145
EVANS 127
David 184
James 196, 259
Orlanda 121
Septimus 37, 52, 128, 136
Triphena 117
William 162
EVARTS
Alfred 172
Charles 172
George 162
William 243
EVENDEEN
John 222
EVENDEN
Charles 221
EVENS
Sylvester 257–8
EVERET
John 162
EVERTS
A. 221
Branch 208
Rinaldo 169
EVERETT 264
E. D. 167
Ebenezer 169
Eliza 167
EVETTS
Jared 218
EWELL 92, 200
EWER
Eleazer 212
EWING
Thomas 155
William 23
EWINGS
Alexander 114
EWINS
George 104

F

FABER
J. P. 108
FACER 120
FA-E-DA-O-QUA (Jones) 16
FAHLEY
John 140
FAILING
Walstein 104
William 57, 104
FAIRBANKS
A. 108
Eleazer 61

FAIRBANKS (cont.)
Ira 113, 155, 221
Jonathan 148
FAIRBAULT
Joseph 74
FAIRCHILD 217
Andrew 221
David 68, 220, 264
Edward 121
Harrison 218
Jas. 120
Moses 40, 212
Sarah 220
William 222
FAIRCHILDS 24
John 208
FAKE
Warren 105
FANCHER 259
J. W. 195
FANNING
John 17
FARINGTON
DeWitt 144
FARIS 169
FARLEY
George 143
Philip 124
FARLING
Andrew 128
FARMER'S BROTHER 23–4
FARNAM
William 34, 211
FARNHAM
George 205
FARNSWORTH
S. 104
Shubal 184
FARNUM 242
B. W. 108
FARR
Claudius 156
G. Clark 267
FARRER
Asa 258
Ebenezer 225
FARRINGTON
D. C. 90
DeWitt 140
S. M. 140
T. F. 133
FAULKNER 55, 257
FAUROT 96, 159
Henry 82, 115, 160
J. P. 84, 115
Jacob 53, 161
John 159
FAUROTE
Horace 184
FAY 67, 248
Hinckley 177
Marietta 177
FEAGLEE
George 184
FEAGLER
John 218
FELLOWS 209
Henry 52
John 32, 206
Joseph 32, 49, 128
Martin 124
Myron 124
FELT
Jabez f-58, 199, 202, 204

FELT (cont.)
James 200
Mary f-58
FELTUS
Henry 70
FENTON 55
Abram 267
John 157
FERBUSH
Jonathan 258
FERGUSON
D. B. 53
George 184
H. B. 64, 172
Harrison 108, 109
Hester 181
John 153, 158
L. B. 181
Levi 60
Robert 181
Stephen 153, 158
W. M. 170
William 124, 181
FERO 258
FERRIS
David 181
Harvey 172
I. 170
FERRY
Gideon 116
William 269
FIELD 78, 128–9, 221
David 18, 130, 136
George 78
Henry 66
P. H. 77–8
Perez H. 52, 65, 77
Peter 52
Timothy 34, 61, 102
William 130
FIELDS
Edwin 233
Erastus 233
James 34, 111
Lucius 124
FIERO 145, 147
Abraham 155
Alonzo 172
Elizabeth 155
Hannah 155
Isaac 172
Magdalen 146
Mary 155
Nelson 162
Oliver 157
Peter 155
Sidney 162
William 146
FILLOTT
Ann 181
FINCH 44
Albert 255, 258–9
Charles 157
Darius 255
S. B. 256
Samuel 256
Tobias
W. H 166
FINK
George 163
FINLAY
Alexander 140
FINLEY
Alexander 123, 213

FINLEY (cont.)
Marshall 110, 117
Robert 155
FINN
Calvin 204
James 157
John 157
FINNEL 205
FINNEY 259
Charles 61
FISH 35, 264
Alexander 147
Elizabeth 235
Ephraim 189
James 19, 101–3, 114, 190
Josiah 40
Zuriel 178
FISHER 204, 232
A. G. 239
C. E. 220
Charles 108, 157, 201
Christian 30, 153
Franklin 124
George 156
Hannah 241
Henry 140, 184
Isaac 232
Jno. 124
John 15
Nathanial 239, 241–2
FISK 110, 218
J. 108, 113
John 58
U. M. 243
FITCH 112
Alonzo 217
& Blair 201
Ebenezer 220
F. 241
Ludwick 217
Silva 155
FITZGERALD 82, 181
Theodore 82
Theophilus 120
Walter 160
FITZHUGH 32, 38
Charles 80
William 49
FITZMORRIS
M. 210
Thomas 212
FITZPATRICK
John 233
FITZSIMMONS
John 205
Thomas 223
FLAGLER
Isaac 160
FLAHERTY
O. 182
FLANAGAN
William 123
FLANDERS
George 230
Jacob 229, 230
John 229, 230
FLANNAGAN
Thomas 140
FLANNERY
Patrick 144
FLEMING 114, 117
Robert 262
FLETCHER
A. 30

FLETCHER (cont.)
Charles 268
David 263
FLETCHER
George 224
Looice 242
Martin 268
FLEURER
Charles 203
FLINN
George 143
FLINT
Aaron 34, 111
Andrew 223
Deborah 169
Joseph 224
Millard 64
Rossel 166
William 169
FLOYD 40
FLYNN
George 123
FOGARTY
James 123
FOLES
Cynthia 236
FOLFORD
David 130
FOLER
C. J. 52–3, 66
Charles 51–2
H. W. 52
Mr. 227
FOLLETT
Frederick 18, 35, 154, 159
Oram 66
FOLLEY
Frank 184
FONDA 12
FOOT
Henry 143
Samuel 52, 76
FOOTE
Samuel 51
FORBES 249
Horatio 116
Joanna 34, 250
John 248
Jonathan 249
M. P. 113
FORCE
Isaac 184
Samuel 205
FORD 90, 257
Ambrose 201
Charles 184, 267
Erastus 201
Henry 144, 172
J. W. 113
Theodore 172
FORDON
George 49
FOREMAN
John 184
FORSHAM
Robert 142
FORSHAY
C. 108
FORSYTH
George 82
L. 208
Leander 209
FOSGATE 166

FOSKET
  & Carter & Sackett 118
  H. 159
  Isaac 118
  John 118
  Sophi 117
  Robert 224
FOSMIRE
  & Betts 200
FOSTER 88, 103, 109, 119, 169, 181, 241, 264
  Adrian 184
  Constable 194
  H. T. E. 134
  Henry 64, 65
  I. P. G. 58
  James 124
  Joel 230
  John 111
  Joseph 156
  N. C. 108
  Richard 122
  William 180, 184
FOUNTAIN
  John 157
FOWLE
  W. K. 67, 140
FOWLER
  Ami 217
  D. C. 140
  Samuel 13
FOX 265
  F. 115
  George 227
  Henry 214
  Herman 140
  Hermon 93
  J. 259
  John 249
  Jonathan 258
  Josephus 218
  Polly f-58
  Squire 201
  Zepediah 207
FOY
  Edward 233
  John 156
FRANAWAY 165
FRANCIS
  A. 108
  Ephraim 224
  Frederick 231
  Gilbert 240
  H. 243
  Isaac 243
  Jeremiah 124, 172
  John 142
  Maria 242
  Moses 158
  Rebecca 242
  Sally 242
  Sarah 246
  Stephen 240
  William 124, 240, 242
FRANCISCO 38, 153
  Francis 259
  Harrison 259
  Jacob 255
  M. A. 56
  Michael 160
  Samuel 157
  Thomas 249
  W. H. 140
FRANEY
  A. P. 168

FRANK
  Peter 157
FRANKISH
  F. 152
FRANKLIN 84, 85, 90, 95–6
  A. 228, 229
  Benjamin 20
  House 104, 108
  John 228
  William 20, 254
FRARY
  Eleazer 230
  John 230
  Kirby 230
FRASIER
  John 166
FRAZEE 67
  Charles 213
  Robert 213
FRAZER
  Ann 167
  Benjamin 108, 120
  Horace 167
  John 123, 199
  & Moul 200
  William 124
FREDERICK 160
FREELAND
  August 124
  Henry 123
FREEMAN 104, 119
  Benjamin 256
  Charles 124
  Huldah 35, 190
  John 119
  Warren 254
  William 172
FREER
  George 122
  Robert 124
FREMIN 33, 197
FRENCH 66, 87
  Alexander 201
  Andrus 144
  Clara 218–9
  Darius 230
  Ebenezer 207
  Freeman 266
  Hiram 205
  Jabez 114, 262
  Jesse 43
  Joseph 268
  Laura 219
  Louisa 218
  Lyman 140
  Moses 140
  Sarah 218
  Seward f-212
  T. D. f-208
  T. H. 167
FRENY
  Elezaer 225
  John 225–6
FRESBEE,
  White & Company 166
FRESHORN
  John 148, 159
  W. J. 159
FRESHOUR
  Charles 144
  Henry 143
FRICKER
  George 172

FRIES
  Catharine f-172
  David f-172
  Sarah Robison f-172
  William f-172
FRINK
  M. 161
  Marshall 195
FRISBEE 228
FRISBIE
  Brothers 258
  Marvin 255
  William 172
FROST 163, 227
  Eli 203
  Ephraim 250
  Jacob 226, 250
  Jonathan 250
  Lewis 242
  Moses 250
  Stephen 228
FROSTER
  William 146–7
FRUSHOUR
  Charles 140
FRY
  Jacob 157
  William 184
FULLER 225, 265
  Benjamin 258
  David 220
  George 222
  H. H. 212
  Josiah 258
  Levi 178
  M. 209
  Mortimer 123
  Myron 168, 172
  Otis 263
  Reuben 157
  S. W. 203
  Samuel 232, 264
FULMER
  James 184
FULTON 129
  Hugh 146
  Isabella 65
  J. S. 146
  James 140
  John 34, 149
  Joseph 146
FURLONG
  Frederick 143
FURMAN
  Charles 204
FURNER
  Arthur 124
  Thomas 184

G

GAGE 120
  Almon 109
  Amasa 153
  C. 116
  Caleb 115–6
  Charless 121
  Darwin 93
  E. D. 140
  Frank 105
  George 116, 243
  John 116
  Marion 153

GAINES 181
   Frederick 124
   George 234
GALINEE 197
GALIVAN
   John 140
GALLAGER
   James 142
GALLAGHER
   John 196
GALLIEU 254
GALLUP
   Wm. & Co. 199
   William 199
GALPIN
   L. Q. 265
GALUSHA
   Clark 172
   Elon 113
GANIARD
   Peter 18
GANNETT
   Charles 249
   H. B. 250
   Lewis 249
GANNON
   Abram 157
   Michael 179
GANSON
   James 25
   John 19, 25
GANSON'S SETTLEMENT 54
GANT
   John 184
GANTZE 134
GANUNG 255
   Asa 255
   Edward 255–6
   John 255
   William 257
GANYARD
   Peter 241
GAP
   Joseph 143
GARANGULA 10
GARDENER 209
   Perry 221
GARDINER
   Hannah 220
   Harvey 93
   P. 220
   Peregrine 220
GARDNER 95, 167, 241
   Benjamin 17, 101
   C. C. 181
   E. W. f-125
   Elisha 192
   George 196
   Harvey 244
   Ishmael 115
   John 216
   Lucinda 35, 216
   P. 19
   Peregrine 216
   Rensselaer 172
   S. P. 31, 192
   Samuel 24, 102, 114, 143
   William 44
GAREY
   Rufus 253, 257
GARIETY
   Patrick 162
GARLICK
   Thaddeus 70

GARLINGHOUSE 266
   Benjamin 229
   Charles 121
   J. 53
   John 229
   Joseph 41, 53, 227
   L. B. 104
   Louise 227
   Mary 227
   N. 131
   Nelson 227, 232
   S. B. 106
   Stephen 263
GARLOCK
   Charles 172
   Dwight 172
   Gardner 184
   George 172
GARNET'S MILL 56
GARNIER 33, 197
GARRETSON
   G. J. 134
GARRETT
   V. L. 169
GARRISON
   Aaron 212
   Abraham 153
   L. B. 116
GARROW
   Nathaniel 57
GARTHEN
   Jno. 234
   William 234
GARY
   Alpheus 248
GASKILL
   Asa 201
GATCHEL
   W. H. 193
GATES 103, 109, 154, 218, 232
   A. G. 218
   Abel 233
   Alfred 184
   Amos 218
   Benjamin 168
   Betsey 168
   Curtis 218, 220
   Cyrus 16, 163
   Daniel 17–8, 79, 101, 154, 159, 163, 218
   David 116
   Edwin 96, 157
   Elijah 168
   Elisha 159
   Esther 163
   Fordys 163
   George 168
   Gideon 227, 232
   Horatio 154
   J. Spender 159
   James 146
   John 159, 243
   Joseph 159, f-160, 163
   Lewis 223
   Marvin 216, 218
   Mary 159
   Melaneton 219
   Milcah 163
   Moses 163
   Pamelia 163
   Parley 154
   Rachael 168
   Solomon 146–7
   W. W. 166
   William 172

GATIS
   Samuel 249
   William 249
GAULT
   James 65
GAUSS 210
   Benjamin 206, 209, 212, 230, 239
   Thayer 209, 212, 230
GAVOTT
   John 70
GAY 96
   James 161, 232
   William 142, 149
GAYLORD
   F. S. 264
   Flavial 155, 207
   Frederick 172
   Levi 112
   John 140
   Moses 207
   S. B. 105
GEACHALER
   Andrew
GEARING
   Frederick 194, 196
GEDDIS
   John 91, 121
GEIGER
   Frederick 122
GELDER
   Barney 140
GELSON
   M. B. 264
GELSTON
   Miles 264
GEORGE 170
   James 166
   Lewis 154
GERATY
   Patrick 123
GERMAIN
   Rollin 82
GERRUM
   Charles 124
GERTEL
   John 157
GERVIS 168
GETCHELL
   John 172
   William 194
GEVIN
   John 124
GIBBARD
   Isaac 170
GIBBIN
   Hugh 222
GIBBS 254
   Daniel 220
   W. M. 108
GIBSON 57, 179
   Frederick 144
   H. B. 56, 57, 90
   Henry 28, 57–8, 76, 104, 107, 111
   John 149
   Richard 161
GIBSON BLOCK 166
GIDDINGS 115,l 117
   Cynthia Orme 179
   Joshua 112, 117, 181
   Linus 228
   Richard 115, 179, 181
   William 234
GIDDINS
   William 251

GIDDIS
J. B. 92
GIFFING
George 133
William 130
GIFFINY
George 140
GIFFORD
A. C. 170
E. H. 170, 175
Emmons f-166
Isaac 257, 264
John 170
Joseph 201
N. A. 115
GILBERT 129, 255, 262, 265
C. L. 231
Calvin 172
Candace 231
David 248
Deacon f-80, 230
Edwin 228
Elias 40, 49, 225–6, 231
Ellis f-80
Haskell 254
Horace 227
John 66, 124, 205
Joseph 217, 220, 225, 231, 244, 247, 255
L. 255
Oscar 244
Polly 231
Porteus 86
Rachael 220
Reuben 231, 248, 254, 257
Seevel 248
William 257
GILBERTSON
William 158
GILES
Charles 156
GILL
Joseph 266
GILLEM
John 192
GILLESPIE
James 77
GILLET
Anna 176
Asa 176
Asel 176
Clark 204
Harvey 204
Joab 176–7, 180
Joel 113, 118, 176
John 176
Lydia 176
Ruth 176, 188
Sarah 176
Ziba 176
GILLETT 57
Amasa 160
Charless 162, 182
Horace 267
& Hubbell 105
Jacob 181, 241
Joab 18, 193
Josep 18
L. H. 219
Liddy 118
Miles 44
Milton 119
Seymour 263
Thos. 44
Zacheus 204

GILLIS
David 191
Enos 199, 202
James 199, 204
John 191
Naomi 203
Robert 200
Samuel 198–9, 202–4
GILMORE 97, 259, 266
James 113, 169
GINAUT
George 205
GINTHER
Peter 184
GIPPLE
Henry 222
GISBORN
Thomas 144
GITTENS
John 172
GLADLE
Robert 251
GLAND
Levi 147
GLASGO
John 143
William 143
GLASGOW
John 142
GLEASON
Bezaliel 36, 176, 178
Charles 184
Esther 148
Joseph 120
GLEN
Henry 12
GLENN
Thomas 184
GLOVER
David 218
Oliver 116
GODDARD 256
Daniel 223
GODFREY
Charles 49
Ira 58
GODWIN
Hiram 122
GOFF
Charles 249
Isaac 221
John 34, 168
Samuel 243
William 130
GOLD
David 193
GOLDEN
James 184
GOLDSMITH 79
B. M. 112
GONG
George 184
GOODALE 119, 177
Alanson 169
Charles 244
George 172, 184
Horace 182
S. 113
Silas 172, 184
Solomon 34, 62, 113, 168, 211, 240, 242
GOODALL
S. 34
GOODELL 118
Ezra 165

GOODELL (cont.)
Nathan 263
GOODENOUGH 203
GOODING 109, 208, 238–9
Asahel 241
Chester 213
Edward 241
Edwin 238
Elnathan 18, 238–9, 240–1
Ephraim 242
G. 56
George 18, 118, 241–2
Horace 213
James 18, 239, 241–2
Job 240
Lydia 241
Manning 107
Spencer 53
Thomas 240
Timothy 118
William 18, 110, 113, 211, 238, 240–1
Zephaniah 240, 244
GOODING'S HOTEL 55
GOODMAN
Wm. 51
GOODOW
Jefferson 143
GOODRICH 218
A. 259
Abner 256
Billings 266
Charles 190
Elijah 257
Griffin 219
James 268
Jason 262
John 267
Luther 266
Peter 268
GOODSELL
Daniel 225–6
GOODWIN 128, 136
Charles 143
D. 127
Daniel 63
James 17, 225
Manning 64
W. H. 109, 113, 132
Wells 117
William 51–2, 64, 108, 170, 232
GOODYEAR
C. H 158
GOOLD
Niel 234
Solomon 119
GORDEN
C. 127
E. 127
GORDON 44, 120, 127
E. H. 128
Elijah 136
George 229
James 157
L. 200
Samuel 124
GORHAM 79, 103, 127
G. 64
George 64
Judge 78, 108, 118
N. 56
Nathaniel 13, 15, 17, 21, 25, 31, 38–9, 44–5, 47, 53, 58, 78–9, 101, 105, 107, 235
William 16, 49, 66, 105
GORHAM MILL COMPANY 153, 155

GORMAN
    John 184, 195
    William 196
GORMLEY
    James 124
GORSE
    Esther 242
    Samuel 242
GOSS
    Benjamin 18, 35
GOULD 17, 164, 218
    A. F. 207
    Allen 255
    David 203
    Henry 221
    James 33, 66, 102
    Jeremiah 14
    John 201–2
    Luther 255, 259
    Lydia 255
    Martha 49
    N. & Co. 104, 107
    William 254–5, 259
GOULD PLACE 207
GOUNDRY
    George 32, 129
    Thomas 32
GOWERS
    James 259–60
GRACEY
    William 140
GRACY
    J. T. 181
GRADY
    Thomas 105, 140
GRAFF
    Jno. 205
GRAG
    Joseph 30
GRAHAM
    Adelbert 223
    Franklin 140
    Guy 213
    James 195
    William 222
GRANBY 257
GRANDIN
    E. B. 42
    J. L. S. 156
GRANDY 259
GRANFIELD
    John 184
GRANGER 36, 81, 102, 106, 110, 178, 229–
    30, 249
    A. 108
    E. L. 140
    Elihu 17–8, 164
    Erastus 44
    F. 49, 56
    Francis 38–9, 41, 52, 57, 64, 80, 104, 107–
    8, 115
    G. 108
    Gehazi 178, 181
    Gideon 20, 38–9, 49, 51–2, 82, 103–4,
    117, 250
    Gordon 164
    Hiram 184
    J. N. 53
    J. Albert 42
    John 57–8, 104, 108
    Julius 81, 178
    Pierce 17–8, 164, 168–9
    Sarah 178
    Schuyler 257

GRANT 91–2, 95–6, 98, 100, 119
    Charles 207
    Joseph 263
    Loring 113, 132
GRAVENDIUSH
    Vincent 124
GRAVES 246
GRAVILER
    John 161
    Lewis 163
GRAY
    Abby 236
    Charles 140
    George 236
    Henry 172
    James 95, 163
    Maxwell 236
    Peter 146
GREEN 82, 90, 97, 103, 198
    A. M. 132
    A. W. 113
    Arnold 258
    B. F. 227
    Benjamin 254, 256
    Byron 52
    Charles 108, 266
    Cynthia 227
    & Delano 119
    Emily 116
    Erastus 153, 157
    Eugene 223
    G. H. 153
    H. 257
    Henry 153, 192
    Ichabod 263
    Isaac 96, 226, 234
    J. L. 231
    J. R. 166
    Jacob 157
    James 228
    Jeremiah 254
    John 24, 165, 224, 228–9, 230–1, 248, 256
    Kelly 50
    Moses 235
    Richard 168
    S. 131
    Sarah 235
    Solomon 140, 156
    Staats 52
    Sylvanus 144
    Thomas 140
    W. 207
    William 143
GREEN'S STORE 103
GREENE
    John 81
    Jonathan 249
    S. 77
    William 77
GREENFIELD
    David 143
GREENLEAF
    M. A. 110
    S. & Company 55
    Samuel 42, 55, 107
GREGG
    A. H. 58
    Augustus 184
    Frank 184
    Hugh 227
    John 159, 242
    Leslie 184
    Mary 242
    R. R 53

GREGORY 140
    Chas. f-144
    Daniel 224
    E. S. 57, 105, 110
    Elijah 105
    G. 108
    Harry 161
    Henry 70, 74
    Hubbell 221
    J. G. 64
    J. J. 64
    James 221
    M. M. 229
    O. H. 133
    Philip 146
    Willard 150
    Willis 115
GREGORY'S STORE 105
GREIG 16, 24, 103, 107
    J. 49
    John 26, 32, 38–9, 42, 49, 51–2, 56, 58, 64,
    79, 104, 106, 111, 115, 136, 160, 247
GREIVES
    John 67
GREY
    Alfred 199
    B. B. 149
    H. 166
    Henry 170
GRIDLEY
    S. H. 112
GRIER
    James 123
GRIERSON 98
GRIEVE 136
    Walter 69, 128
GRIFFAS
    John 122
GRIFFEN 129
GRIFFES
    John 267
GRIFFETH
    C. 217
GRIFFIN 218
    August 204
    John 58
    Wheeler 219
GRIFFIN'S BATTERY 85
GRIFFITH 217
    David 169
    Elias 222
    Griffith 130
    J. W. 166
    John 224
GRIGGS
    Peter 172
    Stephen 172
GRIMES 114
    Charles 115
    H. N. 108
    Hollister 121
    N. 59
    N. & Son 105
    Paul 262, 263
    William 59, 179
GRINNELL
    Gideon 191
    Hester 266
    John 191, 204
GRISSET
    Wealthy 169
GRISWALD 106
    E. A. 93
    S. 200

GRISWALD (cont.)
    Solomon 202, 204
GRISWOLD 241
    Darius 211
    E. A. 262
    Edgar 267
    Elijah 200
    George 124
    Levi 169
    Solomon 200, 202
    Timothy 157
GROAT
    Jno. 124
GROSSBECK
    Hannah 155
    John 53, 156
GROSVENOR
    Godfrey 136
GROUT 255, 257
    Catharine 254
    Israel 169
    Justus 254–5, 259
    Loring 169
    Martha 254
GROVE
    William 30
GROVER
    Charles 221
    Joseph 34, 61, 231, 241
GUE
    Benjamin 82
GUERNSEY 33, 152
    James 53, 79
GUIFFORD
    R. B. 166
GUION 83
    G. M. 85
    G. Murray 93
GULICK
    Henry 120
    J. G. 132
    John 153
GULLY 199, 202
GUNDERMAN
    James 244
GUNN 210
    Clarissa 211
    L. B. 104
    Linus 118, 209
    Martha 211
    Moses 206, 209, 210
    W. P. 104
GUNNING
    William 129
GUYANT
    Huldah 203
    William 204

H

HAAKER
    Francis 184
HAAS
    Frederick 130
HACKETOFF
    Albert 124
HACKETT
    George 184
    Thomas 124
    William 184
HADLEY
    E. A. 266
    Elder 258

HADSELL
    Tobias 184
HAGER
    A. W. 38
HAHN
    F. B. 108
    Thomas 66, 109
HAIGHT
    Benjamin 194
    W. E. 140
HAINES 259
    B. 258
    Sanford 123
HAIR
    D. 108
HALDEN
    Cornelius 255
HALE 74–5, 169
    Benjamin 74, 77
    Charles 223
    E. 111
    Ebenezer 58, 104, 107
    Henry 223
    Isaac 43
HALE BLOCK 105
HALL 41, 44, 147, 150, 216–7
    A. B. 130
    Abraham 130
    Abram 132, 136
    Alex 124
    Amos 17–9, 40, 44, 51–2, 54, 78–9, 212,
        216–7, 220
    Augustus 217
    Charles 143
    D. S. 73
    David 216
    E. 259
    E. S. 80
    Edward 147, 147
    Enoch 216, 218, 219
    Ephraim 177
    H. B. 219
    H. S. 82
    Heman 216
    Henry 142
    Hiland 218
    Isaac 124, 218
    J. C. 58
    James 113, 218, 255
    John 50, 104, 107, 136, 172, 250, 268
    Johnson 255
    Joseph 221
    Margaret 147
    Mary 220
    Morris 216
    Moses 60, 130, 136
    Myron 217, 220
    Nathaniel 165
    Owen 110
    Philemon 217, 220
    Philip 184
    Phoebe 220
    Samuel 130
    Thomas 53, 110, 147, 216, 218
    William 58
HALLETT
    Charles 135
    J. W. 127, 129
    Jacob 49, 129
    Thomas 258
HALSEY
    Charles 80, 81
    Silas 169

HALSTEAD
    Hiram 123
    Thomas 155
HAM
    John 172
HAMBLIN
    Edwin 264
HAMILL
    S. S. 203
HAMILTON 198, 230, 228
    Charlotte 236
    D. L. f-225, 229, 230
    D. Leonard 232
    D. T. 218
    David 229, 236
    E. C. 58
    Hosea 149
    Hugh 229, 236
    Isabel 236
    Jefferson 155
    John 144, 169
    Justin 229, 236
    N. R. 104
    Polly 236
    R. 257
    Reuben 256, 258–9
    William 229–30, 236
HAMLIN 208
    Edward 184
    Elijah 18, 208, 215
    F. W. 211
    H. W. 59
    Haskaline 214
    Henry 215
    J. S. 208
    James 215
    Mary 208, 215
    Olive 208, 218
    Philo 18, 208–9, 212, f-215, 215
    Sylvester 230
    William 211, 212
HAMLINE 170
HAMMOND 105, 132
    A. 132
    Arthur 132
    Frank 168
    Hugh 167
    Israel 155
    R. H. 140
    S. H. f-67
    Stephen 51–2, 129
    William 123
HAMPSHIRE
    George 184
HAMPSON
    John 56
HAMPTON
    Andrew 258
    Generla 98
    James 258
HANAHAN
    John 205
HANCE
    Benjamin 193–4
HANCOCK 83–4, 91–2, 100, 229, 255
    G. S. 233
    R. T. 120
    Robert 232
HAND
    A. J. 180, 181
    Alfonzo 172
    Sarah 113
    William 142, 172
HANDY 216, 220

HANDY (cont.)
Daniel 220
Samuel 216, 220
Sarah 220
HANES
John 172
HANEY
Charles 214
Francis 213
HANFLIN
James 143
HANFORD 201
HANKS 157
HANLEY 156
Hiram 208
HANNA
A. J. 160
James 157, 180
William 180, 182
HANNAH
John 115
HANNON
George 162
HARBINGER
N. 124
HARBO
Fritz 123
HARBRIDGE
Thomas 142
HARDENBURG
John 127
HARDENBURGH
John 14
HARDIN
Benjamin 263
HARDING
Stephen 43
HARDY
John 143
L. 168
HARFORD 146
Charles 25
HARGEN 166
HARGER
Henry 170
Milton 170
HARKNESS
James 231
LeRoy 156
HARLAND
James 49, 181
HARLIT
George 124
HARLOUGH
James 182
HARMER 22
HARMEY
Robert 172
HARMON 225–6
Abel 231
Byron 185
C. 181
C. E. 166
Carlos 181
George 132, 152, 169
John 124
M. P. 146
Nathaniel 231
W. P. 140
HARPER
George 268
HARRINGTON
Ahab 190
Ella 177

HARRINGTON (cont.)
Israel 35, 177, 180
Lucretia 177
Mary 177
Nathaniel 177
Thomas 177
HARRIS 97, 145, 191, 145, 257, 262
Alba 257
Alonzo 267
Ambrose 266
Charles 148
Daniel 208
Francis 154
George 267
Heber 257
Hiram 242
James 57, 261
Jenkins 269
John 14, 19
Joseph 234
Levi 266
Martin 42–3
Patrick 140
Silas 207
Thomas 140
HARRISON 39, 165, 180
John 49
HART 88, 116, 199, 203, 257
Albert 184
C. 129
C. B. 121
Chauncey 200
David 163, 177, 184
Ella 177
Ellery 177
Harvey 202
Huldah 113
Jabez 200, 202
James 140
Jeremiah 177
Joel 123, 160, 230
John 159
Jonathan 107
Joseph 132, 148–9, 177–8
Orville 124
R. 52
Reuben 52, 58, 63, 203
Robert 177, 184
Selah 148
T. E. 110
Theodore 102
Triphena 200
Truman 52
V. O. 264
William 57, 157
HARTELL
Charles 184
HARTSON
Asa 258
HARTWELL 49
Ephraim 229–30
John 49
Moses 255
HARVEY 219
Asahel 66
Benjamin 193
J. 212
James 219, 221
Jewett 219
John 224
Lydia 255
Robert 144
Sarah 221
Simpson 193

HARWOOD 153
Eben 152
Newton 140
HASKALL 110
HASKELL 120
Edson 50
Eli 113, 119, 266
Ely 242
Gilbert 50
HASKIN
Abel 119
HASKINS
Alonzo 172
Amos 191
Charles 172
James 191
John 191
HASMON
George 113
HASTINGS 89, 136
Horace 132
Perez 77, 130
HATCH 248
Ann 249
Charles 248
Edwin 213
Frederick 244
George 248
John 213, 248
Lucy 248
Luman 248–9
Lyman 248
Nathan 241, 247–8
Nathaniel 18
Thomas 248
HATFIELD
Levi 155
HATHAWAY
A. C. 211, 242–3
Esther 195
Franklin 123
H. A. 242
Isaac 18, 181, 189–90, 192–4, 202
Joseph 195
Lorenzo 191–2, 194
Mary 242
Otis 192
Perez 49
Robert 17, 189
Thomas 15
HATTON
William 123
HAVEN
Hiram 144
HAVENS 221, 259
HAVERLAIN
Michael 162
HAVERLIN
Michael 123
HAWES
Judith 263
Lyman 242, 262, 264
HAWKINS
David 251
Horace 251
Jeremiah 199, 203
Timothy 180
W. F. 199, 201
William 223
HAWKS 228–9
A. 170
B. F. 170
C. Seymour 172
Cephas 165

HAWKES (cont.)
D. R. 53
Dexter 228
Eleazer 165
Eleazor 170
Joseph 165
Robert 172
S. C. 165-6
HAWLEY 203, 207
A. 199
Abner 199, 202
Asa 118
Comfort 130
Curtis 230
David 117
Enos 18, 112, 117
Eric 202
Gideon 72
Henry 117
James 53, 199
& Little 104
Manley 202
Punda 118
Thomas 200, 202-3
William 172
HAWS
C. W. 217
Lyman 228
HAWVER
Allen 184
Joseph 184
HAXLEY
Charles 143
HAY
Philip 132
HAYDEN
Aaron 165
Liberty 161
Russell 162
HAYES 40, 91, 214, 247
Harold 246
J. B. 53, 108
Joseph 112
M. 251
Maria 246
Mumford 214, 247
P. 106
Patrick 196
Pliny 214, 246-7
Ralph 214
Richard 201
Richmond 246
W. E. 130
HAYNES
Amos 221
HAYS 92, 210, 218
Arnold 115
James 130
Lyman 115
M. 210, f-210
HAYTON
Asher 121
William 105
HAYWARD 209
A. J. 108
Asa 209, 211
Caroline 110
H. 108
Holloway 110
Stephen 190
Theodore 193
W. P. 130
HAYWOOD
Thomas 184

HAZELLIN
William 184
HAZEN
Celia 235
Edward 36, 225, 230
Henry 230
Isaac 228
Lemuel f-80
Paul 230
HAZLETT 229
See also Heazlett
HEACOCK 118
Aaron 17
Noah 117
HEAGHT
Eli 233
HEALY
Henry 143
HEARD
John 251
William 251
HEATOR
John 173
HEAZLETT
A. B. 257
George 259
Ledrey 260
Sedrey 259
HEAZLIT
Eli 222
HEBARD 259
HEBBARD
E. 132
HECKMAN'S BRIGADE 93
HECOX
Aaron 119
Asa 18, 198, 211
Gillis 118
Mary 211
Miles 119
Vine 198
HEDDING 170
HEDGAR
Charles 52
HEDGES
Decatur 267
HEFFRON
Michael 173
HEINER
Henry 205
HELMER
F. D. S. 166
HEMENWAY
C. G. 248
HEMENWAY PLACE 249
HEMINGS
Anthony 130
C. L. 130
HEMINGWAY
Charles 110
Julia 110
HENDEE
A. & Co. 217
Ariel 52
Charles 218-9
Stephe 219
HENDERSHOT
Benjamin 124
HENDERSON
James 158, 230-2
Richard 262
HENDRICKS 259
Electra f-235
S. 109

HENEHAN
Thomas 199
HENEY
Sylvanus 182
HENIKE 153
HENION
Thomas 200
HENNESY
Arthur 123
HENNESSY
Edward 163
Michael 163
HENNIGAN
William 142
HENRY 60, 253
D. Fernand 82
David 132
Fanny 167
G. R. 160
James 235
John 136, 140
Moore 122
Nelson 160
Paul 132
Samuel 233
William 268
HEODLEY
Henry 221
HERALD
Moses 184
HERBENDON
George 123
HERENDEEN 81, 91, 132
E. 108
Edward 53, 189
G. F. 192
George 108
Gideon 192, 194
Joshua 25
Lemual 132
Lydia 178
N. 194
N. C. 190
Nathan 18, 177, 189-90, 193
Orin 90, 195
Thomas 190
W. 194
W. A. f-98
W. W. 190
Welcome 189, 193
HERINGTON
Welcome 35
HERLING
Henry 213
HERMAN 221
Simeon 172
HERMANS
Charles 212
E. J. 161
HERRICK
Edward 218
Henry 120
Joshua 257
Nathan 257
HERRINGTON
Caleb 230
Joshua 190
Welcome 189
HERRON
David 124
James 33, 60
William 124
HERSEY
S. C. 182

HERSEY (cont.)
Sylvanus 173
HERSHEY 156
W. 207
HESLOP
J. 127
HESSELGESSER 262
HETH 96
HETON
T. G. 196
HEWETT
Henry 124
Samuel 49
HEWITT 250
Elisha 256
Fryphene 220
Henry 258
J. 258
James 258
John 26, 220
Robert 144
Theodore 124
William 140
HEWLITT
Dewitt 133
HEWMAN
Eliza 154
HIBBARD 170
F. G. 113, 132, 170
Henry 221
Nathan 261
S. 218
HICKEY
James 123
John 140
HICKLEY
Edward 122
HICKOK
H. H. 256
S. R. 257
HICKOX 41, 217
Asa 199, 202–3, 206–7, 212
B. H. 169
Burton 70, 74, 111
Candice 125
Eunice 125
George f-76, f-94, 117, 125
H. H. 258
Henry 125, 208
James 112, 125–6
John 34, 111
Levi 117–8, 125
Luman 125
Mary 125, 219
Michael 125
Orpha 125
Polly 203
Reuben 232
Roxana 125
Stphen 125
William 185
Zophar 125
HICKS 232
Aaron 211, 240, 242
Benjamin 53
Catherine 242
Ed. 166
Edward 173
Edwin 53
Eleanor 242, 247
Elias 194
Elizabeth 242
George 173
Jabez 241–2, 257

HICKS (cont.)
James 123, 173
John 214, 242
Jonathan 242
Lucy 242
Martin 248
Nathan 227, 232
Otis 211, 242
P. F. 242
Peleg 243
Scott 53
W. H. 248
W. L. 53
W. Scott 242, 246
Walter 143
William 144, 173, 249
HIER
Jesse 143
HIGANBOTHAM 209
HIGBY
Elisha 49, 160
HIGGINS
David 211
Edward 123
Rody 121
S. 256
Samuel 163
Stephen 254
William 131
HIGHAM
Robert 57, 106
HIGHT
Benjamin 120
HIKOK
James 50
L. P. 64
HILBORN
A. R. 231
HILDRETH
James 184
John 165
Spencer 49
Samuel 55, 106, 166
W. A. 108
W. M. 167
William 49, 52–3, 109, 165–6
HILL 96, 156
A. 156
Byron 173
Charles 107
Cyrus 250–1
David 16
Eleazer 239, 241–2
Eli 52, 232
Ephraim 178–9
Erastus 228–9 247, 250
Eva 159
G. C. 182
Gregory 201
Henry 177, 186
James 142
John 244
Joel 159, 179
Joseph 79, 154, 157
Melvin 174
Michael 123
Myron 143
Robert 118, 211–2
William 201
HILLARD
M. L.182
HILLERMAN
Reuben 140

HILLHOUSE
Thomas 51–2, 58
HILLMAN
Reuben 162
HILLS
Abram 123
George 112
Henry 243
Hezekiah 239
HILT
Pamelia 170
HINCKLEY
Guy 263
Harriet 266
J. W. 264
John 263, 274
HINDMARCH
Ed. J. 140
HINMAN
Chester 155
HINTON
Jerome 173
HINTONTA 271
HIPPLE
George 133
HITCHCOCK 226
Amanda 119
J. C. 212
Lyman 256
M. 116
HIXON
James 163
HOAG 247
George 192
James 192
Wilbur 113
S. 218
HOAGE
Walter 161
HOAGLAND 257, 259
Henry 259
J. B. 259
James 255–6
HOARD
Menzo 144
HOBART 68–70, 72–3, 111, 232
Clarence 212
J. H. 72
John 70, 135
HOBBEY
C. E. 169
HOBBIE
Robert 140
HOBSON
J. W. 207
HODGE
Charles 234
H. L. f-214
Isaac 184
Lewis 217
HODGES
Amos 123
Lewis 218
Raymond 124
Elsa 212
S. S. 212
HOFF 166
William 122
HOFFMAN
Martin 180
Michael 140
HOGAN
Jno. 124
John 157

HOGANS
  Benoni 256
  Hiram 255–6
  Samuel 255–6
HOGARTH 77
  R. 128
  Richard 52, 77, 130, 136
  W. 133
  William 132
HOGEBOOM
  James 154
  V. 154
HIGLE
  John 120
HOLBROOK
  C. H. 168
  Daniel 143
  Lewiss f-168
  Rufus 194
HOLCOMB
  Amanda 266
  Ann 266
  Asahel 267
  Electa 266
  Eliza 118
  Eunice 117
  Frederick 249
  H. 209, f-210
  James 251
  Keziah 249
  Perry 262
  Seth 112, 117
  Winthrop 249
HOLCOMB FARM 181
HOLDEN
  Cornelius 256
  John 266
HOLDREN
  Clarissa 253
  Jacob 229, 253, 263
  Samuel 253
HOLDRIDGE
  George 194
  Josiah 192
HOLEMAN
  L. S. 140
HOLLAND 116
  Adam 124
  Isaac 124
HOLLENBECK
  A. S. 130
  Cornelius 229
HOLLET
  P. 156
  Peregrine 60
  Perry 155
HOLLEY
  Andrew 148
  Myron 24, 32–3, 37, 41, 45, 49, 51–3, 66,
    79
HOLLIDAY 146
HOLLIHAN
  James 213
HOLLISTER
  Edwin 210
HOLLMAN
  Henry 144
HOLLOWAY
  Peter 209
HOLLOWAY'S TAVERN 209
HOLLY
  Myron 107
HOLMES 120, 208
  Daniel 232

HOLMES (cont.)
  E. H. 170
  E. M. 203
  Lucy 168
  M. W. 168
  Martin 169
  Mary 228
  Robert 124
  Rufus 173, 184
HOLSTEIN
  Henry 75
HOMER
  Frank 184
  William 49
HONEYWELL
  Daniel 257
HOOD 91–2
  A. H. 130
HOOKER 83–5, 91
  Allen 241
  Horace 241
  John 262–3
  Joseph 176
  Richard 253, 263
  Samuel 129
  Thomas 262
HOOKER'S STAR CORPS 90
HOPKINS 209
  B. C. 220
  Caleb 52
  Clark 149
  Crosby 143
  Ehud 209, 211
  Elisha 209
  H. 166, 173, 217
  H. H. Mrs. 166
  Hannah 211
  Harrison 218
  Jennie 166
  Peter 195
  Pitts 210–1
  S. W. 133
  Squire 209
  William 205
HOPPOUGH 259
  David 253–4, 258
  Decker 254
  Halsey 254
  M. D. F. 255
  P. 255
  Peter 254
  W. G. 254–5, 258
HORNBY TRACT 257
HOOLCHAN
  James 124
HOOP
  Adam 13, 20
HOOPER 92
  John 147
  Joseph 162
HOPPEN
  Wiliam 157
HOPPER
  Andrew 162
  George 266
  Milo 222
  William 157
HORN
  John 122
HORNBY
  J. 127
  John 20, 127, 247
HORNSBY
  Thomas 182

HORTON
  Cornelius 167
  Ebenezer 30, 31, 192
  Elisha 251
  George 67
  John 142
  Samuel 140, 173
  Thomas 205
HORTSEN (See also Houtfen, Houten)
  William 69, 128, 135
HOSFORD 168
HOSKINS
  Geoerge 220
  J. D. 180
  J. G. L. 113
  Leonard 249
HOSMER 26, 79
  Frederick 78
  George 162
  Timothy 39, 52, 63, 78–9
  William 170
HOTCHKIN 220
  James 61, 220, 266
HOTCHKISS 165, 248, 250
  Albert 244
  Augustus 216–7
  Alice f-58
  Daniel 119
  Fannie f-58
  H. A. 243
  H. R. 216
  Hiram 244
  J. H. 217
  Jacob 80
  L. B. 165–6, 170
  Leman f-58, 166, 180
  Lucinda 216
  Lucretia f-58
  & Mc Loud, Smith, Snow 166
  Mortimar 251, 268
  Nathan f-58
  Selma 119
  T. O. 166–9
  Thaddeus f-58, 166
  William f-58, 169
HOUGH 168
HOUNSON
  F. 140
HOUSE
  Abel 160
  E. 203
  John 32
  Sarah 32
HOUSEL 262
  Charles 122
  David 124
  Jasper 120
  Joseph 124
HOUTEN
  W. 127
  Wm. 128
HOUTFEN (Hortsen)
  Wm. 129
HOVAR
  E. 170
HOVEY 228
  Ebenezer 108
  Jacob 155, 220
  Mary 155
  Solomon 40
HOWARD 129, 202
  Alexander 182
  Anson 184
  H. 180

HOWARD (cont.)
Henry 49, 108, 120
J. 257
O. R. 132
HOWE 80-1
Abigail 167
Henry 49, 79-80, 83, 115
J. Q. 166
John 53, f-170
F. S. 169
Joel 199, 202
Milton 167
S. S. 118
Samuel 80
Thomas 167, 213
William
HOWE'S DIVISION 85
HOWELL 15, 24, 28, 32, 38, 79, 103, 181
A. P. 108
A. W. 66, 85, 110
Alex 53, 105
Farley 143
Gilbert 52
John Greig 80
M. H 127
N. W. 58, 79, 102, 105-7
Nat. 52
Nathaniel W. 24, 32, 37-9, 44, 49, 52-4, 66,
78-80, 106-7, 129, 159
& Parrish 105
T. M. 37
Thomas 38, 52-3, 64, 107
HOWES 79
Benjamin 212
Charles 124, 213
Henry 214
Robert 213
HOWLAND
Benjamin 180, 192
Betsy 178
Charles 178
David 178, 180-1
Elizabeth 178
George 192
Gilbert 176, 178
J. A. 185
Jedediah 257
Joab 193
Job 178, 192-3
Jonathan 178
Laban 259
Labin 257
Nicholas 49, 178, 180-1
Polly 178
Samuel 257
HOWLANDS 178
HOWLETT 67
HOYT
E. D. 198
Lockwood 167
HUBBARD
Almira 254
Foster 173
Henry 149
Hiram 43, 108
Homer 204
Isaac 184
J. E. 207
P. 160
S. 256
Silas 264
Susannah 112
HUBBEL 24, 66
George 168

HUBBEL (cont.)
& Gillett 105
Levi 51, 108
Lucas 169
Mary 110
W. S. 42
Walter 32, 38-9, 41, 49, 52, 54, 58, 76, 80-1,
102-3, 107-8, 112
William 41
HUBBELL BLOCK 105
HUBER
William 140
HUDNOT
Justin 258
HUDSON 221
Alexander 196
& Brother 105
David 52, 69, 73, 106, 128, 136
Isaiah 201
J. G. 105
Jacob 124
Samuel 116
HUESTIS
Jonathan 169
HUFF
Allen 258
John 255
Moses 255
Reuben 258
Timothy 255
HUFF'S 259
HUGER 84
HUGGINS
James 181
HUGHES
Charles 145
Erastus 201
John 142, 199-200, 202
R. 127
Richard 135
& Sargent 201
W. 212
William 204, 220
HUGSON
L. 249
HUKE
George 140
Hattie 160
John 160
HULBERT
Henry 184
Lorinda 225
HULBURT 39
Burton 205
John 207
Marcus 205
Warren 266
HULBUT
Millard 124
HULL 116, 147
Ambrose 78-9, 129
Calvin 166
Jeremiah 202
Lorin 206
James 256
Moses 60
S. P. 67
HULSE
Henry 124, 251
James 244
Lester 119
HUMPHREY 207
Charles 164, 168
John 158

HUMPHREY (cont.)
Jonathan 207
Oliver 148, 164, 168
Roswell 207
HUMPHREYS 18, 91, 201
HUMPHRIES
Charles 205
HUMPHRY
Betsey 169
Robert 169
HUN
Thomas 241
HUNN
Isaac 241
Nathan 118
Thomas 34
Zadoc(k) 32-4, 61, 111, 118, 203, 211, 220,
241, 264
HUNT 59, 217, 241
Aaron 230, 253, 263
Armenus 266
Aarthus 222
Edmund 82
Elston 201-2
Erastus 217
Jane 253
Judson 143
Ralph 217
Stephen 222, 223
HUNT'S HOLLOW 263, 265
HUNTER 97
Joseph 124
HUNTINGDON
Charles 224
HUNTINGTON
E. A. 112
E. G. 170
Frank 224
George 140, 223
Israel 52
Robert 218
Sidney 219
HUNTLY 228
HUNTLEY
C. L. 108
Elias 119
Frederick 223
Ralph 119
HUNTOON
Asbrah 184
HURD
David 119
Edgar 53
Elijah 117-8, 154
W. H. 248
Walter 107
HURLBURT 147
Alvin 222
E. G. 249
James 43
Russell 205
HURLEY
Cornelius 199
HUSBANDS
George 123
HUSSEY
Alexander 222
John 217
HUTCHINS
E. M. 77
HUTCHINSON 221
George 173
H. 217
William 259

HUXLEY
    Sarah 169
    Sally 169
    Thomas 169
HYATT
    E. R. 109
    Reuben 192
HYDE 109
    C. F. 234
    Caleb 254, 256
    Charles 257-8
    Daniel 143
    Edwin 184
    George 149
    Henry 108
    James 256, 258
    John 161
    Joseph 259
    Lucian 184
    Merton 184
HYLAND
    Andrew 266
    John 259, 266
HYLLER 256

I

IDE
    Henry 143
    John 129
IMBODEN 97
INGALLS
    William 219
INGERSOLL 207
    Elijah 202
    Elisha 200, 203
    Erastus 202
    Thomas 202
INGRAHAM 259, 266
    A. 248
    A. S. 121
    Abel 255
    Andrew 244, 255-6, 258-9
    C. O. 243
    Charles 244
    Chauncey 250
    David 250
    Ebenezer 255, 258
    Eugene 213
    George 269
    H. 266
    Hiram 256
    Ira 182
    J. 242
    LeRoy 124
    Lorenzo 255-6
    Lucy 258
    P. 248
    Richard 249
    William 246
INGREHAM
    William 143
INGRAM 118
INSEE
    Boswell 88
INSSE
    Boswell 244
    Gregoire 96
    Gregory 244
    T. 243
    Tellisphor 244
INSON
    George 124

IRETON
    Thomas 140
IRISH 34
    Daniel 62, 168, 242
    David 176, 211
    L. 181
IRONS
    Jeremiah 34, 168
IRVIN
    Pierce (Pierre) 135
    Theodore 75
IRWIN
    James 244
    John 124
    William 184
ISBELL
    Lyman 242
ISENHOUR
    Leonard 145
ISHAM
    William 124
ISRAEL
    Joseph 119
IUNSSE (See Insse)
    Illesphor 122

J

JACKAWAY
    Levi 184
JACKMAN 254
    Belinda 254
    Josiah 254, 257
JACKSON 38, 67, 75, 83, 85, 90, 98, 107
    Abner 75
    Azer 241
    Daniel 241
    E. 108, 127, 242
    Elias 129, 241
    John 184
    Josiah 49
    Mary 107, 161, 170
    Oliver 41
    Sidney 178, 186
    Wellington 244
    & Whitewater 106
    Wm. 82
    William 184, 202, 242
JACKSON'S CORPS. 87
JACOB 79
    N. 63, 111
    Nathaniel 64, 79
JACOBS
    Albert 200, 205
    C. & Co. 200
    Calvin 17, 225, 238, 239
    Harriet 110
    Levi 33
    Meyer 130
    N. 111
    Nathaniel 63, 76, 111
    Samuel 130
JACOBUS
    Charles 264
JAMES
    Amos 160
    Ishmael 263
    Richmond 182
    William 263
JAMESON
    Hugh 44, 52, 114, 117, 119
JAMISON
    James 116

JANES 170, 235
JAQUES
    C. S. 263
JARED
    Stephen 18
JARVIES
    Elijah 146
JARVIS
    H. N. 49, 108
JASON
    John 230
JAY 36
    Peter 68
JEFFERSON 39
    Hamilton 113
    Thomas 52
JEFFREY
    Charles 190
    Frederick 81
    Henry 196
    Robert 173
JEMISON
    Mary 15
JENKINS 13, 227
    A. C. 221
    Edson 143
    Elisha 45
    Emma 30
    Jora 223
    J. F. 107
    Jeremiah 107, 111
    John 17
    Nathaniel 60
    W. M. 107
    William 258
JENKINSON
    M. 130
JENKS
    Amos 33, 148, 169, 203
    Benjamin 189
    Bortle 213
    & Bushnell 193, 199-200
    Edmund 189
    George 190
    Nathan 199-200, 203-4
JENNINGS 15, 127, 144
    Charles 192
    Clark (Elark) 127, 129
    Hiram 53, 181
    J. N. 253
    Lark 16
    Lemuel 24
JENNY 24
JENREE
    John 30
JENSEN
    James 214
JERED
    Joel 176
JEROME
    Amasa 111
    Charles 244
    Edward 244
    John 232
    Theodosia 200
JEROMES
    Jonathan 226
JERSEY
    Benjamin 257
JERVIS
    K. P. 113
JESSUP 100
    William 99, 162

JEUDEVINE
  Hannah   110
  William   102, 108
JEWEL
  Joseph   203
JEWELL
  Frederic   81
  Joseph   33, 60
JEWETT   64, 147, 228
  H.   64
  Harvey   53, 59, 65–6
  Henry   243
  John   143
JOCK
  John   233
  Walter   233
JOHNS   41
  Evan   56, 80, 107, 112
JOHNSON   83, 98, 219, 242
  Abraham   173
  Alonzo   196
  Amos   264
  Asa   207, 211–2
  Beals & Tiffany   104
  Benjamin   171, 264
  C. F.   158
  Charles   117, 123
  Cornelius   255, 259
  Daniel   204
  David   140, 184, 162
  E.   92
  Elisha   180
  Fistus   143
  Frank   218
  Garrett   184
  George   157, 195, 227, f-230, 237, 244,
    267
  H. A.   58
  I. N.   58
  J.   108
  J. B.   264
  J. R.   203, 243
  Jacob   244
  James   121
  John   55–6, 108, 123, 140, 144, 163, 173,
    241, 261–3
  Joseph   140, 144, 173
  Larnard   241
  Lewis   173, 255
  Luke   256, 257
  Luman   269
  Lyman   142
  Miner   143
  Nancy   256
  Nathan   173
  Oliver   117, 244
  Robert   143, 158
  S. K.   129
  Sylvester   237
  Thomas   258
  William   35, 49, 67, 93, 104, 108, 143, f-174,
    184, 254–5
JOHNSON BLOCK   105
JOHNSTON   22, 92, 99–100
  J.   129
  John   32, 127, 129
  Thomas   169
  William   25
JOHNSTONE
  Ellis   135
  John   21
JOLLY
  T.   161

JONES   97, 109, 130, 144, 159, 166, 168, 241,
    266
  A.   53
  A. G.   241
  A. J.   109
  Amos   52, 159–60, 228, 254, 257
  Andrew   159
  Asa   240–1
  B.   208
  B. W.   66
  Charles   124, 267
  Davis   244
  E. W.   144
  Ebenezer   228
  Edward   244
  Elijah   143, 240, 243
  Elizabeth   159
  Ephraim   241
  Eva   159
  Ezra   148, 149, 242, 244
  Fernando   80
  Frank   163
  George   268
  Harriett   148
  Harry   256
  Henry   148–9, 255
  Horatio   15–7, 22, 24, 36, 127
  J. S.   207
  Jacob   143
  James   163, 179, 266
  Jennings   144
  John   15–6, 101, 159, 268
  Joseph   124, 191
  Leonard   240
  Myron   116
  Nancy   178
  Nathan   177
  Paul   173
  Peleg   239
  Rebecca   159
  Richard   159
  S. A.   242
  Seth   240
  & Swift   107
  Solomon   109
  Susan   159
  Sylvanus   241
  T.   257
  Thomas   136, 159
  Warren   124
  William   15, 168
JOPSEN
  Mark   210
JOQUES   33
JORDAN
  John   122
  William   123
JORDON   95
JOSELYN
  Charles   30
JOSEPH
  August   184
JOURDAN
  Robert   129
JUDD
  Bethel   68
  Jonathan   68
  Levi   149
  Mary   177
  Patrick   140
JUDEVINE   230
  Harry   229
  William   229

JUDSON
  Philo:251
JUNE
  William   173
JUPITER
  Benjamin   173

K

KAIMBELIN
  John   242
KALAHER
  James   140
KANALY
  Patrick   195
KANE
  James   234
  Peter   124
KANOUSE
  Ezra   173
KARNEY
  Orrin   184
  Reward   118
KAUFMAN   248, 250
  William   248–9
KAY
  Richard   204
KEARNEY   87
  Ravard   111
KEEGAN
  James   234
KEEN
  Frank   144
KEENE
  Frank   173
KEENEY
  Jonathan   130
KEHOE   99
KEITH
  Michael   263
  Nelson   140
  Richard   140
KELLER
  Jacob   123
  John   122, 162
KELLOGG   208
  Erastus   167
  H. H.   149
  Joel   210
  John   160
  Sylvester   219
  T. H.   132
KELLY   166, 256
  Catharine   256
  George   140
  Henro   105
  James   173, 229, 256, 259
  John   105, 121, 256, 259
  Jno.   124
  Lawrence   140, 173
KELLY'S GROCERY   166
KELSEY   132
  A.   52
  C.   110
  Camp   38
  E. S.   132–3
  James   33, 169, 203
KEMPTON
  Frank   143
KENDALL
  Henry   207, 211
  Jno.   211

KENDRICK
William 220
KENNARD
John 167
KENNEDY
Adam 234
John 35
Patrick 162
William 108
KENNEY
Charles 142
KENNICOTT
E. D. 136
KENT 24, 38
Abigail 240
Ansel 178, 181
Celeste 246
James 45
John 240, 246
Moses 178
P. 240
Phineas 53, 240
William 169
KENTFIELD
William 124
KEOUGH
Lawrence 184
KERSEY
William 55, 66
KERSHAW
J. 109
KETCHAM
Germond 191
N. 198-9
KETCHUM 159, 258
Jared 202
Joshua 202
Smith 184, 195
KEYES
B. W. 130
Benjamin 144, 209
Generla 88
John 79, 206, 208, 210
Nelson 144
Thaddeus 17, 206
KEYES CORPS 87
KIBBE 38
Edward 261, 263-4
Eli 262
May 264
S. T. 107
Sally 263
William 48, 102, 108, 110, 116
KIBBOURH
Luman 218
KIEHLE
Daniel 81
KILBOURN
Joseph 114, 148
KILDAY
Michael 121, 184
KILMER 166
A. 67
KILPATRICK 98
KILVEA
R. 115
KIMBALL 258-9, 264
Betsey 254
Ebenezer 253-4
Heber 201, 204
Ira 254, 259
Vilate 201
KIMBEL
May 242

KIMBER
Geo. 113
James 243-4
Thomas 194
KIMBERLIN
John 60
KINCAID
Joseph 60
KING 166, 209, 210
Belmont 143
Eli 169
Elisha 140
Fred 56
G. C. 169
Gardiner 161
George 259
Gideon 18, 210
Hugh 110
J. 259
J. D. 169
John 57, 149, 259, 267
John S. & Company 58
Joseph 124, 211, 259
Moses 209
William 119, 167
KINGSBURY
Hiram 203
J. 209
KINGSLAND
Edward 129, 135
KINGSLEY 38
Ambrose 256
Camilla 256
E. C. 43, 106
Joseph 169
Lucy 258
Thomas 181
KINGSLEY'S HOTEL 106
KINKAID 166
KINNE
Elias 230, 264
Peabody 263
KINNEY 24, 116
Alanson 256
John 256
Patrick 184
Richard 256
KINYON
Gilbert 228
Samuel 233
KIPP
George 124
H. D. 140
Harrison 162
Henry 90
James 58
KIRK
H. C. 167-8
Hiland 157
Hyland 53
KIRKLAND
Samuel 12-4, 16, 23
KIRSCH
Zervias 140
KISDALE
Frederick 142
KITCHEL 259
KITTREDGE
Hosea 155
John 185
KLEBER
Jacob 162
KLUV
Gustavus 143

KNANER
Adolph 233
KNANERE
E. F. W. 233
KNAPP 113, 159, 167-8
Amos 159
Cassius 162
David 159, 229-30
Ebenezer 257
Edwin 213
Ezra 160
Franklin 160
Henry f-162
J. S. 140
James 163
Jared 159, 181
John 205, 222
Leonard 160-1
Samuel 257
Thomas 158
William 124, 205
KNEELAND
A. S. 113
KNICKABACKER 160
KNICKERBOCKER
David 249
Eleazer 219
Larry 249
Orpha 249
William 268
KNIFFEN 168
William 205
KNIGHT
David 13, 185
Richard,130
KNOCKERBOCKER
William 122
KNOWLES 249, 258
Albert 123
Daniel 256, 259
Eber 124
F. G. 255
Jared 254
Marcus 233
Margaret 255
Mary 194
Raynolds 196
Seth 254-5, 258
KNOWLTON
Michael 205
Sarah 214
KNOX 16, 22, 51, f-80, 101
Isabel 236
KOBB
Lewis 158
KOEHLER & STOKOE 155
KOHLWAY
William 185
KOLLER
Nicholas 185
KOOMER 153
KOUTZ 99
KRONKHITE
John 202
KUSHER
Jno. 124

L

LACEY 60
Edgar 269
W. B. 156
William 33, 60, 72

LACKEY
  S. J. 169
LACOST
  Edward 158
LACY 242
  B. 60
  Frank 268
  Phenenonine 268
LADD 201
  Hiram 197, 199, 201
  John 203
LADEW
  Jacob 143
LADU
  Betsy 168
  James 168
LA DUE
  C. W. 180
  Jacob 140
LA FAYETTE 42, 107, 128, 129
  George 129
LAFLIN
  John 141
LAGE
  Franklin 223
LaHIR
  Patrick 143
LaHOUTON 206
LAIDLAW
  James 141
LAIGHT
  Henry 128
LAKE BREEZE HOUSE 104
LAKE
  David 196
  G. H. 153
  Henry 208
  Julia 126
  William 142
LAKER
  Edward 124
LAKEY 38
  James 38
LAMAN
  A. G. 156
LAMAR 84
LAMB 256
  Austin 69
  Frederick 124
LAMBERTON 210
  John 210
  Reuben 103, 116
LAMONT 259
  Charles 222
LAMPHERE 217
LAMPHRIE
  John 144
LAMPORT
  John 53
  William 49, 52–3, 109, 110, 112–3, 157
LAMPSHIRE
  M. B. 140
LAMPSON
  Nathaniel 191
LA MUNION
  Amy 178
  Philip 178
LANCASTER
  Robert 158
LAND
  Hiram 182
LANDON
  Joel 50

LANDOR
  J. A. 200
LANE
  Addison 185
  Ishmael 170
  James 200
  John 200
  Michael 124
  Timothy 200
  Williadm 141, 144, 230
LANES 230
LANG
  William 185
LANGDON
  A. S. 120
  Martin 130
  Thomas 86, 141
LANGWORTHY 89
LANING
  George 130
LANNING
  Ralph 169
LANSFORD
  Babitt 156
LANSING 112
LAPHAM 58, 177
  Abraham 189, 194
  Anson 178
  David 176, 187
  E. G. 38, 42, 59, 85, 103
  Elbridge 235
  Eldridge 51–2, 82, 109, 116
  Epiphras 177
  Ira 194
  Isaac 59, 176–7, 181, 192
  Jared 177
  John 52–3, 193
  Joshu 181
  Lucinda 177
  Marietta 177
  Spencer 177
  William 57
  Zimroda 190
LARHAM
  J. W. 140
LARKINS
  James 161
  Thomas 218
LARNARD
  Erastus 160
  William 160
LARNER
  Mary 30
LARZELAERE 129
  See Luzalere
LA SALLE 197
LATHAM 154
  Charles 110
  Henry 162
LATHBURY
  John 182
  Thomas 182
LATHROP 230
  Albert 124
  Louisa 169
  Thomas 195
LATHUR
  W. 129
LATIMER
  Ebenezer 170
LATTA 146
  J. 127
  S. 127
  Samuel 129, 149

LATTING 115
  Hart 181
  Jacob f-162
  John 115, 187
LATZ
  Nicholas 124
LAUGHLIN
  W. 166
LAURENCE
  Archy 242
  Samuel 53
LAVELLE
  Patrick 185
LAVEN
  James 140
LAW
  Thomas 185
LAWRENCE
  David 143, 256
  Ed. 108
  Edward 148
  Elbert 146, 148
  H. Clay 90
  Henry 122
  Joshua 185
  M. D. 148
  Samuel 52, 130
  T. A. 166
LAWS
  William 142
LAWSON
  Conrad 163
  Edward 185
  G. 127
  James 130
  Loton 204
LAWYER
  Joseph 158
LAYNE
  William 229
LAZELERE
  Richard 135–6
LAZENBY
  John 162, 173
LEACH
  Alfred 233
  Elisha 219
  Jacob 52
  Norton 143
  Payne 219
  Richard 52
LEACOCK
  Samuel 61, 160
LEAD
  William 185
LEARY AND BACHELOR 199
LEAVENWORTH LOT 109
LEAVY
  William 53
LEDLIE 100
LEE 82–5, 88, 90–4, 96, 98, 100, 157, 182, 204
  Arthur 12
  B. 169
  Charles 223, 266
  Dennis 266
  Elias 263
  Elisha 13, 206
  F. 52
  Francis 162
  George 210
  Gideon 49, 52
  Henry 121
  J. H. 111
  James 262

LEE (cont.)
Jesse 169
John 163, 250, 263
Jonathan 261
Joseph 160
Joshua 52
LaFayette 120
Louisa 220
Leiphart 249
Orin 268
P. 212
Phineas 35, 249, 262, 265
Reuben 216, 220
Reynold 212
Samuel 204, 205
Seth 215
Sherman 147
Thomas 45, 248–9
William 217
LEECH
Porter 218
LEESAN
Wm. 148
LEESON
May 150
LEFFINGWELL
C. S. 111
LEGGETT
John 254
LEGORE
Isaac 104–5, 106
Jennie 28
John 268
LEGRO
Lewis 144
LEIPHART 249
LEISER
Frederick 105
LELAND
A. O. 108
Oscar 173
LEMMONS
Moses 182
LEMON
Bernard 213
J. S. 232
LE MUNION
William 185
LENAHER
William 163
LENARD
Isaac 232
LENNON
Bernard 123
LENT 212
William 196
LENTWELL
Lawrence 143
LEONARD
Asaph 57
Erastus 159
LE RUE
Francis 255–6
LESLEE
Benjamin 230
LESLEY
James 163
LESLIE
Jonathan 118
William 124
LESTER 38
Albert 51
George 109
Ralph 53

LETTS
M. 266
LE VASSEUR 129
LEVERE
Daniel 159
George 159
LEWIS 15, 217
Arthur 130, 147
Benjamin f-74
Betsey 202
Butler 254, 256
Charles 223
Daniel 52–3, 128, 135–6
Darius 202–3
E. B. 109
Ebenezer 154
Elnathan 108
Erastus 140
George 65, 185
H. 259
Henry 121, 185
Hosesa 157
J. S. 77, 129
James 154
John 38, 159, 269
Joseph 77–8, 268
M. 59
Martin 40
Melancton f-74, 199, 203
Nathaniel 40, 159–60
Palmer 259
Seth 119
Sylvester 203
Valentine 211
William 143
LIANCOURT
Duke 102, 262
LILLIS
David 144
LILLY
Alva 155
Charles 122
LINCAS
Alonzo 122
LINCOLN 82, 92
A. S. 105
Abraham 263
Agjutant 92
Artemus 114
C. S. 261, 263–4
Cyrille 52
Lucius 249
Otis 153
Sarah 30, 253
Spencer 90, 121, 267
T. L. 249
W. E. f- 247
Wm. 82–a, f-247, 249
LINDLEY
David 223
LINDRUFF
J. 153
LINDSLEY
Abiel 61
John 61, 169
LINES
Edwin 105
S. V. & Sons 105
LININGER
John 143
LINNELL BLOCK 105
LIPPETT
Hezekiah 191

LISCOMB
B. C. 104
LISK
D. A. 180
Margaret 150
LITCHULT
John 173
Julius 173
LITTLE
Charles 63, 109
& Hawley 104
Norma 179
Thos. 141
LITTLE BEARD 22
LITTLE TURTLE 22, 23
LITTLEJOHN
Augustus 61
LIVERMORE
Edward 211
LIVINGSTON
Brockholst 26
John 12–3, 16
Robert 63
LOBDELL
Jacob 17, 198, 202, 204
Joseph 258
LOCKINTON
John 143
LOCKWOOD
F. 141
James 163
LOGAN
Bernard 122, 233
John 244
Michael 158
Patrick 124, 233
Peter 244
LOGIE
Charles 143
LONEY
James 213
Thomas 213
LONG
A. S. 119
Charles 124
James 123, 144, 234
John 143
Sarah 167
LONGSTREET 91, 98
LOOFBOROUGH
Nathan 113
LOOK 67
J. B. 67
LOOMIS 38, 153, 154 (See also Lummis)
Benjamin 63
Chester 40, 51, 56, 153–4, f-158
Cordelia 144
G. 191
George 181,193
Hannah f-158
Henry 144
Homer 144
Irene 144
Jerome f-96, 144
Joab 209
Joram 148
Mary 144
Nathan 153
Nicholas 185
Stephen 144
William 49, 52, 144
LOOPER
Henry 162

LOPER
Henry 173
LORD
E. 115
S. 250
LORKER
Joseph 144
LORMER
Joseph 63
LORRIGAN
Patrick 173
LOTES
Amos 218
LOTHAM
William 233
LOTHROP
Alvan 81
LOUGHBOROUGH
N. 60, 203, 207
Nathan 60, 202–3
Sarah 203
LOUGIE
Alfred 141
LOURISON
James 173
LOVE
Charles 173
J. W. 132
LOVEJOY 44
W. W. 243
William 173
LOVELAND
James 259
LOVELL
George 166
LOVERIDGE 249
LOVET
John 205
LOVETT
Charles 185
Joseph 185
LOW
Antony 241–2
Charles 173
Edward 263–4
George 202
James 162
LOWELL
Maria 168
LOWLER
Andrew 141
LOWN 166
Henry 124, 251
LOWRE
C. H. 67
LOWRIE
N. S. 155
LOWTHROP
Thomas 69, 128, 136
Thomas & Company 69
LOYD
John 219
LOZUIR
John 143
LUBBOCK
Robert 223
LUCAS
Asa 257, 258
John 258
Zebina 119, 122
LUCKER
William 259
LUDLOW 133

LUM
D. L. 130
Daniel 132
Matthew 130
LUMBARD
Lewis 192, 194
Samuel 196
LUMBER
Peter 124
LUMMIS
J. 127
Jerome 129
LUNG
A. H. 113
A. W. 85
Hooper 118
LUSK
Amos 211
Asahel 201–2
B. F. 201
Christopher 269
David 202
Ira 200
John 202–3
LUTCH
Samuel 158
LUTE
John 219
LUTHER
Calvin 262
Ezra 242
LUZALERE 129
LYBOLT
Leander 173
LYDERMORE
Samuel 141
LYKE
Edwin 185
Jeremiah 187
William 185
LYMAN
M. D. 166
Melvin 221
Orange 232
T. J. 166
LYNCH
Lawrence 104
Owen 157
LYNN
Thomas 220
LYON 107, 206
Abner 264
Alanson 263
Andrew 122
Angeline 266
Brunson 264
C. C. 124, 173
David 201
Eli 211
Ichabod 264
Ira 269
J. J. 64
James 42, 48–9, 107, 121
James 65
John 53, 115
Joshua 263
Lucy 211
M. J. 102
M. R. 109
Octavius 267
Oliver 228
Peter 107
Simeon 18, 37, 64, 263
Thomas 103

LYONS
D. 218
William 124
LYSAIGHT
James 124

M

MAC CUMBER
Andrew 244
MACE
James 233
MACK 168
Elizabeth 220
George 166, 170, 173
John 40, 185, 220
Jonathan 118–9
MACKEY 129
MACOMBER
Daniel 177
E. 257
S. 256
Shepard 256–7
MACUBER
Daniel 160
MACUMBER
Cyrus 258
Enoch 258
George 233
MACY
Richard 141
MADDEN
Timothy 264
MADIGAN
Frank 143
Nicholas 143–4
MADILL 92, 93
MADISON 33
Duty 218
MADOLE
Clayton 158
MAFFITT
Elijah 170
Josiah 170
MAGEE
David 129
MAGGS
Frederick 105
MAGHA
Jeremiaahahh 185
MAHEN
Patrick 123
MAHONEY
Patrick 124
MAIL
George 185
MAJOR
Henry 185
MAKER
Archelius 258
MALETTE
James 67
MALIN
Rachel 15
MALLERY
Samuel 241
MALLISON
Marcus 120, 123
MALLONEY
S. V. R. 109
MALLORY 239
Benajah 15
Joseph 63

MALLORY (cont.)
Mary 125
Samuel 239
Stephen 52-3
MALLERY
Phoebe 241
MALON
Michael 185
MALONE
Peter 157
MALONEY
Daniel 124
MALOY 249
MALTBY
Jerome 269
MALTMAN
John 116, f-118
William 213
MAMHARTZ
John 142
MANAHAN
William 223, 268
MANDERVILLE
William 221
MANDEVILLE 133
Henry 133-4
John 170
MANIX
D. 159
MANLY
Horace 109
Lyman 232
MANN , 135, 256
A. M. 133-5
Arnold 219
Frederick 144, 185
Reuben 256, 257
Robert 83
Whitley 219
MANNEY
Patrick 142
MANNING 129
John 185
Theodore 162
William 144, 173
MANOUGH
William 185
MANSFIELD 84
Alonzo f-216
MANSON HOUSE 77
MANWELL
George 162
MAPES
Isaac 173
Lydia 154
MAR
Daniel 173
MARA
John 222
MARBLE
Aaron 240
G. P. 231
Richard 218
Shubel 116
MARCY
Charles 269
MKARDEW
Frederick 142
MARION
Dudley 37
MARK
William 124
MARKHAM
A. G. 192

MARKHAM (cont.)
W. P. 191
Wm. 52
MARKS 159
Walter 53, 159
MARLEY
Dayton 144
R. B. 166
MARRETT
W. 257
MARSDEN
Charles 185
MARSH 203
Amerilus 241
Ann 227
C. H. 109
C. M. 109
Daniel 205
E. O. 166
Erastus 124, 205
George 173
H. H. 240
Isaac 60, 200-3, 211
Israel 49
Joanna 202
Lucy Newman 200
Marcius 239, 241-2
W. B. 204
Whitely 225
Whiting 226
MARTINDALE'S BRIGADE 86
MARSHALL 96
C. T. 133
George f-62
Horace 158
Jacob 77
O. H. 197, 198
MARTIN 55
Comfort 220
David 233
E. W. 113
Edward 234
Edwin 161
Isaac 217
Jacob f-162
John 143, f-253
Lucinda f-226
Nelson 213
Norman 163
Sarah f-253
Spencer 88, 121, 213
William 158, 161
MARTINS 120, 153
MARTIN'S BATTERY 86
MLLARVIN 24, 38-9, 113
D. 56
Dudley 37, 39, 45, 56, 63
Erastus 167
Ezra 216
Jasper 217
Matt 202
Nathan 18, 216
Richard f-58, 167
Sibyl 167
MARY
J. J. 121
Jno. J. 124
Joseph 124
MASON 74, 103, 163
Asa 196
Celeste 246
Chloe 246
Eleanor 246
F. O. 235

MASON (cont.)
Francis 49, 52, f-70, 240, 246
Isaac 241
Israel 214
J. H. 212
John 143-4, 221, 235, 240, 246
Jeremiah 52
Jesse 103, 108
M. 218
Maria 246
& Morse 64
Oscar 240
R. 210
Richard 74, 135
Samuel 190
Sarah 246
W. G. f-196
MASSETH BROTHERS 104
MASSETH
John 122
Joseph 108
MASTER
Abbott 196
Eli 124
George 124
Jackson 142
Nathan;173
MATHER;112
Abner;228
Lute C.;50
MATHEW
John;163
MATHEWSON
Edmond;121
MATOON 264
MATTESON 117
Jacob 53, 108
MATTHEWS 32
Soules & Co. 201
Vincent 21, 25, 32, 38-9, 178
MATTICE
C. M. 105
M. M. 105
Peter 224
MATTISON 68, 132
Abraham 201
Clarence 66
Edgar 122
Elijah 66
J. J. 67, 109
Jacob 66
Jno. 124
Seth 113, 170
William 124
MATTON
F. 116
MATTOON
Henry 121
MAURY
James 123
MAXFIELD
Hiram 52, 263-4
Thomas 263
MAXWELL
H. E. 133
Hugh 13, 20, 101, 148
J. I. 133
T. C. 132-3
T. C. & Brothers 50, 131
Thompson C. 132
MAY
William 161, 205
MAYNARD 51
Holloway 110

MAYNARD (cont.)
John 162
Moses 58
MAYO
Arthur 212
George 204
S. 210
MC ALERB
Alexander 163
MC ALLISTER
William 124
MC ARTHUR
Robert 133
MC BANE 199
MC BLAINE
George 141
Salmuel 141
MC BRIDE
J. W. 109
R. P. 182
MC BURNEY
h. 168
MC CAB
Patrick 141
MC CABE
E. W. 108
MC CALL
D. D. 169
MC CANDISH 147
MC CARE
Michael 233
MC CARRICK
John 254
MC CARTHY
Catharine 30
Dennis 121, 185
James 158
Patrick 123
William 185
MC CARTNEY 242
Bathsheba 242
James 242
William 49, 52
MC CARTY
A. 141
Jeremiah 214
John 143
L. 201
Michael 123
Thos. 205
Westbrook 173
MC CAULEY 177
Amy 146
John 146, 159
Margaret 146
Mathew 146
Rice 146-8
T. A. 148
Thomas 146, 148
MC CLELLAN 82-7, 90, 94
MC CLOSKEY
John 132
MC CLUNG
James 133
MC CLURE 44
Darwin 160
George 228
J. S. 105, 113
James 122
William 109
MC CLURG
James 226
MC COMB
E. 141

MC COMB (cont.)
John 185
MC COMBS
William 141
MC CONNELL
Ichobod 259-60
John 49, 115
MC CORMICK 106
Francis 123
MC COY
David 141
MC CRACKIN
George 169
MC CRAE
John 194
MC CRAY
John 195
MC CREA
John 185
MC CREADY
A. 117
MC CROMB
Polly 242
MC CROSSEN 258
Christopher 232
George 233
Henry 254
James 228
John 258
R. W. 231
Rachel 258
MC CRUM 241
Cornelius 35
MC CULLOUGH
Caddie 40
John 146
MC CUMBER 25
Andrew 251
C. 194
Caleb 194
Charles 251
George 196, 231
John 189-90, 205
MC DANIELS
Joseph 76
MC DERMER
J. 182
MC DONALD 74, 86-7, 135
Angus 51, 77
Daniel 68-74
John 143-4, 157, 185
MC DONOUGH
Nicholas 141
MC DOUGAL 91, 93
MC DOWELL 86
MC ELHANA 242
MC ELHENNY 266
MC ENELLY
James 109
MC FAGGEN 131
MC FARLAND 176, 178
LeRoy 162
MC FRREN
Cassius 143
MC GAFFEE
Peter 268
MC GAREY
Charles 185
James 185
MC GARVIE
Peter 141
MC GEE
Hiram 185
Orrin 124

MC GINNIS
Daniel 156
Millie 235
MC GINTYManassas 185
owen 185
MC GLOON
Anthony 141
Patrick 141
MC GOUGH
Bernard 185
MC GOVERN
John 166
MC GOWAN
Albert 121
James 123
MC GRATH'S BATTERY 90
MC GRATH 87
MC GRAW
Barney 95
Michael 100, 185
Peter 124
MC GREGOR
James 266
T. 116
MC GUE
Robert 120
MC HENRY
Charles 221-2
MC HUGH
John 108
MC INTOSH 99
MC INTYRE
Albert 185, 258
Andrew 123
Samuel 149
T. 116
MC JANNET 264
Robert 68
MC JANNETH
John 50
MC JENNET
David 124
MC KAY
J. 133
MC KECHNIE BLOCK 105
MC KECHNIE BREWERY 106
MC KECHNIE'S HALL 109
MC KECHNIE, J. & A. BREWERY 59, f-86
MC KECHNIE 103
Alexander 59, f-86, 106-7, 117
George 108
James 59, f-86, 106-7
William 109
MCKEE
Abram 257
MC KEES
John 185
MLC KELVEY
James 233
MC KELVIE
W. J. 132
MC KENDREE 170
MC KENNA
Bernard 166
MC KEON
Thomas 185
MC KINNEY 266
James 239, 241, 244
MC KINROTH
C. J. 143
MC KINSTRY
P. 113
MC LAIN
John 185

MC LAREN
D. C.   133
J. F.   133
W. S.   133
MC LAUGHLIN
Silas   144
Timothy   124
William   53, 80
M'LAUGHLIN
William   81
MC LAW   91
MC LAWS   90
MC LEAN
George   203
James   166
William   45
MC LEOD   173
Augustus   169
Donald   259
William   259–60
MC LOUD
A.   166
J. E.   155
Smith, Snow & Hotchkiss   166
MC LOUGH
John   181
MC LOUGHLIN
Silas   123
MC LOUTH   178
A.   193
Draxy   34, 181
G. W.   177
John   176, 193
Lawrence   193
Lonson   193
Marshall   193
Peter   193
T. J.   193
Thomas   52
MC MAHON
Isaiah   170
John   202
T.   199
MC MANN
Hiram   208
James   208
MC MANUS
James   130, 132
MC MASTER
David   146, 219
Luna   212
MC MILLAN
Ananias   191
George   173
Loren   173
Willard   173
MC MILLEN
Ananias   190
Clark   144, 173
Converse   116
Horton   121
MC MYNN
James   195
MC NABB
A.   130
Andrew   130
MC NAIR
Caleb   250
Hugh   52–3
James   84
MC NARA
Thomas   143
MC NAUGHTON
James   141

MC NEIL BLOCK   166
MC NEIL   165
Betsey   167
David   166–7
Robert   80
MC NICHOL
James   131
MC NIEL
David   57
MC NINCH
William   234
MC NUTT
T.   108
Thomas   108
MC OMBER
George   213
MC OSKER
Edward   162
MC PHHERSON   146
Alex   146
Alexander   146
James   141
John   152
Samuel   152
William   146
MC QUADE   132
MC QUAID   149, 212
MC REDMAN
James   143
MC ROBERTS   255
MC VEIGH
H.   108
MC WILLIAMS
Daniel   212
MEACHAM
Randall   66
MEAD   38, 41, 173
Amos   103, 104
Austin   141
Charles   133
Ebenezer   143
Freeman   107
G. W.   168
H. M.   56, 105
Harriet   227
James   144
Jane   153
Jeremiah   155
Martin   213
Sandford   195
Sanford   121
T.   104
MEAD'S HOTEL   56
MEADE   88, 91, 92
MEADON
Charles   213
Thomas   124
MEADS
Israel   263
MEANS
James   147
Joseph   f-142, 147
MEARS
James   149
MEED
Seth   63
MEEK
Benson   115
Charles   111
William   115
MEEMS   129
MEGHAN
D.   196

MELLARD
David   242
MELLISH
Samuel   29, 52, 63
MELODY
Thomas   259
MELOY   253
MELVIN   168
Jonathan   18, 164
MENTOR
Byron   157
Eleanor   169
Hiram   169
MERILL   112
MERELL   132
John   67
MERRICK
Eugene   163
MERRILL   38, 41
A.   133
Andrew   132
G.   152
Ira   42, f-62, 67
J. C.   67
Joseph   160
M. M.   264
Nathaniel   129
S. & Company   67
Sidney   269
MERRILLS
Ira   257
MERRIMAN
Hiram   235
John   123
Patrick   157
MERRY
Ebenezer   78
MERRYMAN
Patrick   143
MERWIN
Charles   155, 204
Isaac   257
MERWYN
John   212
MESSENGER
H. J.   64
Samuel   168
MESSER
Asa   132
MESSICK
Henry   123
METCALF   141
Fanny   263
Fisher   264
Harvey   157
Irving   49
Jabez   18, 262–3
Jacob   263
John   21, 55
Kendric   75
Kendrick   169
METZ
John   141
MICKLE
W. A.   141
MICKS
Alonzo   233
MILBUR & SON   200
MILES   90, 102, 159
Adolphus   122
Alexander   221
Benjamin   122
Charles   162
George   162

MILES (cont.)
Holon 203
Polly 203
S. 136
Stephen 202, 203
MILES' DIV. 96
MILLARD 221
Albert 173
B. T. 264
Channing 224
David 221, 266
Jeremiah 173
Luther 208
MILLER 166, 214, 218, 221, 229
A. D. f-168
Albert 123
Amos 162
Anna f-172
C. S. 219
Carlton 214
Charles 185
Daniel 116
David 43, 147
Edgar 157
Frederick 18, 123
Henry 204
Herman 57
J. 180
James 21, 117
Jerry 119
Jesse 205
John 233
Leeman 53
Lewis 143
Luther 144
Lyman 117
Orin 202
Peter 124
Richmond 106
Samuel 18, 202, 214, 216, 218
Silas 214, 218, f-220, 221
Solomon 218
Stephen 258
Triphenia 113
W. 219
William 124
Wilson 67
MILLER'S
Barn 218
Blacksmith Shop 214
Corners 214, 218
MILLERITE EXCITEMENT 203
MILLETT
O. C. 196
MILLIGAN
William 256
MILLIKEN 68
C. F. 108
Charles 67
Edward 124
N. J. 67
Nathan 53
MILLIMAN
James 255
Nicholas 255
MILLINGTON
Edward 224
S. D. 217
MILLO
George 173
MILLS 168, 228, 258
Charles 158
Elisha 103
Isaac 52

MILLS' HOTEL 56, 106, 109
MINCHELL 242
MINER
Amos Jr. 249
Darius 154
Elizabeth 220
Enoch 241
Martin 220
Samuel 154
Timothy 147
MINOR 216
John 219
Martin 217
Sylvester 181
MINTOR
Eleanor 169
Hiram 169
MISKER
Robert 224
MIX 84
M'KEE
Abram 257
MITCHELL 38
Alfred 123, 245
C. T. 109
C. W. 168
Charles 221
Darwin 124
Ellery 244
Frances 40
George 222
Giles 117
I. W. 257
James 33, 60, 181
Oliver 240
Oscar 196
P. 181
Peter 49, 52–3, 56, 180–1
Theophilus 123, 244
William 181
Zachariah 268
MOFFAT 129, 136
J. 127
MOFFIT
Eline f-74
MOLLET
G. W. 157
MOLLOY
Joseph 222
MONAGLE
Hugh 149
MONEGLE
Oliver 147
MONIER 262
James 49–50, 264
MONROE
Burton 130
Curtis 144, 173
James 173
Oliver 173
MONSON
Joseph 144
MONTAGUE
Elder 113
MONTEATH
J. S. 119
Farm 119
Mill 119
Point 119
MONTETH 60
MONTGOMERY 258
G. W. 182, 242
George 203
& Phillips 155

MONTGOMERY (cont.)
Robert 128
MONY
Silas 231
MOODY
Edwin 124
Robert 147, 148
MOON
Philip 201
MOOR
Hiram 161
MOORE 56, 68, 95, 99
Asahel 198, 200, 202, 204
Benjamin 68, 135
Bruce 198
Caleb 169
Charles 185
Chauncey 111
Clement 70
Edward 162
Enos 49
Eugene 233
Fairbanks 119
Franklin 234
George 39
H. 93
H. G. 66
H. S. 67
Henry 95
Hiram 162,185
Isaac 52, 181, 185
J. B. 141
Jacob 167
James 135, 157, 159, 168, 204, 229
Jane 169
Joel 118
John 141, 167
Luca 169
Lucinda 198
Lucy 169
Oliver 167
R. B. 197, 198
Samuel 201
Sarah 118
Sybil 125
Thomas 122, 123
Timothy 34, 153
W. C. 200
Washinggton 169
William 59, 141, 169, 173
MOOREHOUSE
Jabez 203
MORAN
Patrick 185
Thomas 103
MORE
Thomas 162
MOREHOUSE 259, 262
Jabez 199, 203
Josiah 199, 230
MORELY
Elijah 34
MOREY
A. F. 132, 161, 212
R. H. 207
MORGAN 96, 99, 116, 231, 235
Caleb 108
E. A. 141
Edward 185
Elijah 79
G. D. 231
Henry 264
Hugh 144
James 82, 157

MORGAN (cont.)
    John 257, 264
    Sally 188
    W. A. 141
    William 43, 103, 173, f-235, 254
MORGAN AFFAIR 180, 204
MORISON
    Joseph 96
MORLEY
    Daniel 257
    John 256
MORRIS 22
    Edward 124
    Jacob 80
    Michael 143
    Patrick 123
    Robert 13, 15, 19–20, 31, 47, 78, 127, 136
    Sylvester 259
    Thomas 19, 51–2, 63, 78–9, 102–3, 123, 178
    Timothy 107
MORRISEY
    Thomas 123, 162
MORRISON
    Archibald 144
    Clark 77
    J. 130
    John 143
MORROW
    James 245
MORSE 105, 134
    Antis & Phelps 105
    Antis & Pierce 105
    Chauncy 41, 66
    E. H. 117
    E. M. 64, 102
    Elihu 53
    Isaac 117
    J. H. 105
    L. L. 108
    Legrand 66
    Lemuel 52, 154
    Leonard 152
    & Mason 64
    Orin 119
    Orlander 29
    Orlando 118
    Sarah 113
    Zebadiah 154
MORTON 207, 242
MOSBY'S GUERILLAS 97
MOSEBY 103
    Elijah 104
MOSELY
    Elijah 106
MOSER
    C. P. 170
MOSES
    Daniel 143
    Ezra 143
    William 201
MOSHER
    Charles 169
    George 251
    John 53, 169
    Louis 251
    Sherman 177
MOSHIER
    Charles 161, 224
    John 143
MOSS
    G. A. 109
    George 105
    Nathan 259

MOSSON
    Bachin 158
MOTT 200
    A. 146
    Alice 212
    Allen 157
    Asa 157
    Philanander 169
MOUL & FRAZER 200
MOVIN
    Erastus 170
MOWER
    J. H. 64
    James 53, 107
    John 18, 58, 263
MUDGE
    C. 166
    Charles 166
MUGG 119
MULLER
    C. S. 219
MULLIGAN
    Greig 81
    James 81
    Julia f-62
    Patrick 185
MUMFORD
    George 130
    S. L. 185
MUNCY
    John 86
MUNGER
    Abigail 110
    Bennett 110
    Dwight 80, 108
    George 88
    M. D. 59, 116
    Merrick 109
    Orange 173
    R. D. 212
MUNNELL
    Thomas 144
MUNROE
    Norman 162
    W. 259
MUNSEY
    Jacob 143
MUNSON 91
    A. 49
    Anson 207, 209, 213
    Buel 213
    Charles 212
    Edward 213, 233
    F. 119
    F. E. 92
    Frank 211
    Frederick 209, 212
    Harlow 53, 209, 212
    Harriett 160
    Ira 90
    James 160–1
    Lansing 214
    Ten Eyck 90
    Teneyck 213
    Wililam 185
MURPHEY
    Barnard 157
MURPHY 141
    Adolphus 173, 185
    Charles 124, 213
    Edward 120
    James 161
    John 185
    Joseph 245

MURPHY (cont.)
    Michael 214
    Patrick 185
    William 142
MURRAY 44, 119, 122, 257
    A. G. 108
    Alexander 66
    Alonzo 163
    Elijah 37, 102, 159
    H. C. 109
    Henry 122
    James 142
    John 93
    Reuben 53
    Roswell 201
    Thomas 231, 243–4
    William 159
MURRAY'S INN 160
MURREY 103
MURRILL
    Charles 213, 224
    Henry 213
MURRY
    Electa 160
    Elijah 79
MUSSELMAN
    Michael 166
    Thad. 166
MYATT
    John 124
MYER
    Benjamin 142
    John 142
MYERS
    David 196
    Louis 162
    Luther 259
    P. V. N. 264
MYNDERSE
    Wilhelmus 19
    William 66

N

NAGLE
    D. 128
    David 128, 135
    Patrick 214
NAGLEE 89
NARE
    Henry 144
NARES
    Francis 130
NASH
    Albert 97
NEAFIE
    Amos 120
NEAL
    Moses 173
NEELY
    Henry 75
NEENAN
    Daniel 214
NEFUS
    William 160
NEIGHBOR
    J. W. 68, 141, 166
    John 68, 166
NEILL
    William 45
NEILL'S BRIGADE 85
NEISS
    Louis 173

NELSON
  Charles 185
  Edward 185
  G. 108
  George 204
  H. A. 132
  John 170
  Joseph 163
  O. 203
  Robert 149
  Ruth 167
  & Wing 165
NESBIT 133
NESBITT
  William 149, 185
NESTER 130, f-134
NESTOR 166
NETHAWAY
  James 118
NETTLETON
  Alonzo 143
NEUSTAUMER
  John 196
NEVINS
  J. W. 132
NEWCOMB 109, 167, 263
  Dillis 263
  Silas 263
NEWELL 259
NEWELL 57
  Betsey 167
  Francis 185
  George 143
NEWHALL
  John 164
NEWINGS
  Nehemiah 104
NEWLAND
  C. A. 168
NEWMAN
  A. 154
  A. S. f-107
  George 173
  John 143
  Lucy 200
  Peter 158
  Sarah 155
NEWSON 132
NEWTON
  Amanda 210
  Ezra 160-1
  John 160
  Spencer 162
NICHOL
  Margaret f-62
NICHOLA 115
NICHOLAS 131-2, 135
  G. L. 53
  Gavin 53
  George 52
  John 69, 128, 135-6, 212
NICHOLAS & RICHARDSON 50
NICHOLS 103
  Adam 190
  G. P. 204
  George 219, 245
  J. W. 242
  John 34, 49, 51-2
  Rhoda 30
  Robert 51-2
  Samuel 217-8
NICHOLON
  George 185, 195
  James 141

NICKSON
  C. M. 111
NICKERSON
  C. M. 108
NIHIL
  James 185
NILES
  Charles 222
  David 241
  Reuben 144
NINUS
  L. Bernard 173
NOBLE 167, 228
  Boswick 130
  Elnathan 128
  Levi 228
  N. 58
  Nathaniel 130
  Roger 17
NOLAN
  William 173
NOONE
  Michael 123
NOONEN LOT 109
NORGATE
  John 225-6
  Robert 233
NORRIS
  Charles 173
  E. 40
  Eli 169
  Joel 116
  John 116
  Joseph 173
NORRIS SHOPS 57
NORRMAN
  George 144
NORTH 250
  Alice 212
  C. S. 229
  E. A. 207
  Edwin 126
  Lydia 126
  Morris 259
  Richard 185
NORTHAM
  Charles 173
  Epaphroditus 130
  R. 168
NORTHRUP
  Anderson 258
  Augustus 266
  Chauncey 256
  George 110
  Jabez 258-9
  James 266
  John 223
  Wesley 255
NORTON 107, 169, 207-9
  Aaron 207, 219
  Asahel 34
  D. 259
  Daniel 259
  Diantha 211
  Ebenezer 58, 116
  Eber 40, 114, 199, 206-7, 209
  Elijah 207-8
  Elisha 207
  George 232
  Heman 207
  Horatio 211
  John 228, 255
  Jno. 211
  L. T. 207

NORTON (cont.)
  M. 207
  Marcus 126
  Margaret 126
  Moses 207
  Myron 191
  N. 209
  Nathaniel 52-3, 79, 178, 202, 206-8, 211
  Oliver 211
  Philo 207
  & Richards 102, 104
  S. S. 199
  Sereno 207
  Walter 198
  William 163, 255
  Zebulon 35
NORTON'S DISTILLERY 207
NOTT 120
  A. M. 118
  Alfred 112
  E. 119
  E. S. 118-9
  Epaphratus 119
  James 255
  Samuel 122
  Sarah 112
  Sibley 124
  Valentine 185
NOWLEN
  Asa 55
  Mary 39
NOYES
  Henry 93
  Mr. 129
NUDD
  W. 210
NUTT
  Lyman 255
  Martin 259, 260
NUTT FARM 258
NUTTING
  William 130, 213
NYE
  Albert 191
  Elisha 55

O

OAKLEY 110
  William 263
OAK 22, 24
  Jonathan 18, 148, 168
  Lucretia f-58
  Nathan f-90
  Thaddeus 49, f-58
  William 169
OAKES
  Edward 164
  Fannie 164
  Jonathan 164-5
  Nathan 164
  Thaddeus 164
  William 164
OATMAN
  Edgar 108, 213
  Samuel 122
  Sylvester 122, 213
OBERHISER
  George 220
O'BOIL
  Henry 12
O'BRIAN
  Patrick 176

O'BRIEN
Jno. 124
M. 169
Patrick 123, 143
O'CONNELL
Maurice 157
O'CONNER
John 162
O'CONNOR 169
Edward 182, 212
Michael 163
ODELL
B. F. 165, 166
Lyman 196
Theodore 163
ODELL'S BLOCK 166
O'DONNELL
Michael 205
Patrick 185
O'DOUGHERTY 199
O'DRISCOLL
Michael 158
OFFICE
C. 147
O'FLAHARTY
Edward 144
Martin 221
OGDEN
Benjamin 226
Henry 226, 256
John 158, 132, 256–7
Nelson 232
Thomas 68
O'GORHAM
William 169
O'HARA 38
O'KEEFE 167
O'LAHAY
John 259
O'LAHEY
John 123
OLD 120
OLDER
Morden 213
OLDS
Isaac 181
Sydney 143
OLF
John 157
OLIN
Sarah 30
OLIVER
Michael 259
W. M. 57
OLMSTEAD
Edward 226
Harvey 173
Sophia f-162
OLNEY
Abby 236
David 236, 266
O'LOUGHLIN
Cornelius 123
OMBLER
Henry 141
ONDERDONK
Benjamin 70, 135
H. U. 64
Henry 111
ONDERDUNK 146
A. 146
R. 146
O'NEIL
James 224

O'NEIL (cont.)
T. 226
O'NEILL
Cornelius 214
J. 210
James 234
Thomas 121
O'NIELL
Dennis 222
ONTARIO BANK 107
OPDIKE
C. 131
ORCUTT
A. Carlisle 242
A. S. 219
Aaron 242
Eunice 242
ORDERLY
Thomas 185
ORMAN
George 141
James 141
John 85, 141, 144
ORME
Becky 179
Charlotte 179
Cynthia 179
Harriet 179
ORR
James 1098
Wm. 108
ORRIS
Reuben 79
ORSBORN
William 163
OSBAND
G. 169
OSBORN
Stephen 195
William 258
Wilson 181
OSBORNE
Charles 162
D. H. 198–9
OSBURN 152
Charles 264
OSGOOD
Amanda 178
Amy 178
Barrus 178
Cornelia 160
E. 116
Edward 160, 178
Elihu 178
Myron 178
Thomas 178
Uriah 185
OSGOOD FARM 116
O'SHAUGHNESSY
Thomas 123
OSTRANDER 193
Augustus 143
David 144
OTIS
Joseph 121, 185
OTTLEY 129, 168
Charles 145, 148
Lydia 168
Thomas 52–3, 145
William 49, 168
OUTHOUSE
O. 118
OVERACRE
John 185

OWEN 195
Arming 155
Clinton 259
G. W. 259
George 256
Henry 185
M. 102
OWENS 218
James 116
P. 181
Thomas 173
OYER
Robert 124

P

PACH
Frederick 224
PACK
N. M. 239
PACKARD 240
Anson 49, 242
William 240
PADDEN
William 173
PADDOCK
B. G. 169
Benjamin 113, 156
Charles 122
George 161
PADELFORD
H. f-120
Harvey 50, 82, 120
Henry 53
Reuben 104
Zachariah 116
PADELFORD FARM 116
PADGHAM
David 194
Joseph 194
PAGE
Alfred 132
Charles 141, 157, 185, 209, 210
E. Ransom 112
Edward 144
Grannis 141
Hiram 43
John 170
Samuel 251
W. L. 169
William 224
PAIGE
A. C. 64
PAINE 259
Gideon 193
Parish 162
PALMATEER
Sidney 268
Wallace 268
PALMER
B. 108
Bartley 108
Charles 109
Cornelius 122
E. 157
Edwin 160
George 161, 163, 185
J. W. 53
James 52
Joseph 155
Oscar 185
Sally 235

PALMITER
  N. 170
PARBURT
  George 109
PARCEL
  Ashbel 156
PARCELL
  Isaac 53
PARDEE
  Henry 49, 52
  Silas 200, 202–3
PARENT
  James 124
PARISH
  Susannah 34
  W. S. 115
PARK
  Almeda 242
  Christopher 18
  Joel 18, 241
PARKE
  Moses 180
  Nathan 52–3, 63, 136
PARKER 11, 68, 145, 230, 266
  Daniel 264
  David 158, 251
  E. 129
  Edgar 67
  Edward 160
  Eleazer 249
  Elijah 230–1, 257
  Homer 251
  Ira 53, 67
  J. & Company 55
  James 25, 228
  Jason 19
  John 53, 113, 143, 153, 185, 229
  Jno. 113, 211
  Joseph 160, 210
  Oscar 213
  Pitts 263–4
  Robert 169, 170
  S. 156
  S. H. 128–9
  Stephen 67
  Stiles 60, 230, 250
  Timothy 255
  William 124, 251
PARKHURST
  Marrison 161
  Spencer 162
PARKS 92, 146, 201
  Alexander 146
  Christopher 208
  James 109, 173
  Jerome 267
  Joel 210
  Myron 118
  Robert 147
  Simeon 201–2
  Squier 146, 147
  Sylvester 243
  Ward 241
  William 146
PARMALE 202
PARMALEE
  & Ellis 105
  H. L. 208
PARMELE 218
  Beeby 218
  Charles 212
  Dennis 223
  Edward 108
  Isaac 218

PARMELE (cont.)
  Jno. 223
  Philander 204
  Reuben 34, 61, 199, 202–4, 218, 220
  William 204
PARMELEE
  A. H. 149
  Herbert 148
  James 53
PARMELY 248
  Ezra 249
  James 248, 250, 268
  Warren 248
PARMERLY
  James 49
PARMLEE 115
PARRISH 104
  Anson 249, 266
  Charles 124
  Clara 266
  Edward 53, 108
  Edwin 264
  Elisha 248–9, 250
  F. Drake 248
  & Howell 105
  Isaac 56
  Israel 118
  J. B. 264
  Jasper 16–7, 38, 64, 102–3, 106–7
  Jeremiah 37, 263
  Levi 261, 262
  Lewis 143, 173
  & Pierson 105
  Reuben 261, 262
  Russell 263
  Samuel 261
  Stephen 105
  Warren 108
PARSHALL
  C. H. 58
  Charles 150
  Cornelia 150
  David 118–9
  Gideon 122
  Israel 119
  Jesse 118, 124, 119
  John 122
  William 186
PARSON
  Henry 156
PARSONS
  A. 113
  C. W. 38
  Chester 157
  Daniel 251
  David 212, 216
  Edward 109
  John 173
  Levi 251
  Marcus 52
  Martin 156
  William 211
PARTRIDGE
  Daniel 184
  Dwight 165
  Frank 144
  Grover 187
  John 141
  L.J. 254
  S. S. 166, 168
  Theodore 165
PATCH
  Z. 55

PATHEN
  John 220
PATENCE
  William 20
PATRIDGE FARM 254
PATTA
  John 158
PATTEN
  Geoerge 135
  John 168
  William 49
PATTEN FARM 118
PATTERSON 18, 82
  Abram 257
  Charles 173
  E. 127
  Ezra 40, 64, 129, 148
  J. D. 105
  James 163
  Ralph 144
  Sunderland 150
PATTERSON'S HOTEL 127
PATTISON
  Benjamin 186
  S. 192, 194
PATTON
  George 149
PAUL 108
  Albert 219
  Charles 108
  David 219
  Francis 57–8, 106
  Seth 240
  William 219
  Wilson 267
  Zoroaster 52
PAUL'S DRUG STORE 103
PAULE
  George 211
  Sylvanus 211–2
PAULL
  M. E. 242
  Olive 235
  Willim 235
PAYNE 195
  Allen f-188, 190, 196
  Amanda 196
  Calvin 193
  David 196
  Dewitt 186
  E. C. & Company 155
  Edward 195
  Gideon 190, 193
  Harriet 196
  John 161, 169, 190, 196
  Joseph 143
  M. A. 195
  Marvin 196
  R. W. 232
  Sophronia 196
  Wilson 196
PEABODY 257
  Daniel 257–259
  George 131
  James 155
  John 155
  Selah 160
  Thomas 257
PEACOCK
  Ambrose 123
  Isaac 186
  Joseph 186
  Thomas 186

Index of Names to the 1876 History of Ontario County, New York

PEAKE
John 173
PEARCE
E. 229
Lyman 229
William 163
PEASE
Charles 124
David 168
Edward 124
J. 128
J. and J. 128
Jabez 128, 130
PECK 104, 146, 168, 203, 212, 217, 219
Abner 217
Amos 258
Benj. 212
Clark 49, 212, 216–7, 220
E. J. 80, 167
Elisha 168, 202
Ezra 53, 167, 173
F. B. 218
George 49, 64, 268
Gilbert 233
H. H. 146
H. J. 148
Harriett f-235
Harry 199
Henry 148–9, 174
Hiram 167, 168
Horace 168
Ira 52
Jasper 49, 216, 219
Jesse 168, 263
John 168, 267
Lewis 52, 167
Libbie 212
Lydia 168
Matthew 220
Miranda 49
Palmer 216–7
R. M. 220
Raymond 49, 52, 217, 219
Reynold 220
S. 168
Sarah 168
Seba 168
Silsbe 268
Solon 218
T. 168
Thomas 220, 263
Watrous 219
Whitfield 213
William 66, 201
PEEBLE
Francis 169
PEEKE
A. B. 135
PEER
George 199
PEET
A. L. 199
John 205
PEGLER
George 195
PEIFFER 60
PEIRCE
Betsey 196
PEMBERTON
Cyrus 231
Gates 228
Simon 257
PEMBLETON
Leonard 230

PEMBROKE 160
PENDERGRASS
Thomas 124
PENDRY 266
PENFIELD 38, 103
Daniel 49, 78
H. F. 58, 111
Henry 53, 107
James 254
Jesse 254
PENN
Robie 159
PENNELL 230
A. 229, 236
Abram 232, 235
Abraham 225, 236
Chauncey 225
Caroline 235
Celiad 235
Dennis f-80, 225, 232
Elmira 235
Emeline 235
Epaphras 225
F. G. 225
Fanny 235
Francis 235
Frank 226
George 231, 235
H. 251
Harriet 235
Horace 225, 250
John 225–6, 229, 232, f-232, 235
Lucinda 236
Martha 225
Millie 235
Nancy 225
Sarah f-232, 235
Randolph 225
PENOYER
John 120
Joseph 251
PENTENNY
S. 109
PERCIVAL
James 136
PERKEY
J. 89
Jacob 157
PERKINS 210
Ansil 199
Arnold 204
Charles 243, 245
Deborah 203
Ebenezer 154
Elisha 203
J. 199
Joseph 199, 202
M. 203
Marcus 53
Phineas 248, 250
Samuel 202
Thomas 53, 122
Titus 147
Valentine 147
W. 147
William 144
PERRVEE
Oscar 141
PERRY 76, 102
Asa 263
Asahel 268
Benj amin 186
Daniel 257, 268
Gideon 113

PERRY (cont.)
John 213, 249, 251
Nathaniel 79
Orville 266
Peter 199, 202, 204
W. N. 50
William 68, 75–6, 135, 163
PERRY'S NURSERIES 102
PERSONS
A. 108
Levi 257
PESTLE
John 245
PETERS
Abijah 102, 107
Benjamin 177, 193
Jack 230
Jane 28
PETHORIC
Richard 108
PETITT
John 259
PETSIT
Peter 144
PETTET
Silas 179
PETTIBONE 266
Harvey 263
Stephen 35
PETTIGREW 91
PETTIT
William 52, 154
PETTITT
Franklin 174
PEUEL
Owen 257
PEYTON
R. 134
PHELP 33
Henry 17
Joel 18
Oliver 31
PHELPS 57, 78, 103, 106, 111, 117–8, 135, 166
Ambrose 54, 113–4, 118, 176
D. 225
Davenport 34, 62, 68, 135, 182, 232
E. N. 68
Egbert 67–8
Eliakim 132
Francis 107
& Gorham 117, 247, 261
Joel 114
Jonathan 104, 107
Joseph 115
L. 105
Luke 176
Lydia 113
Morse & Antis 105
O. 107
O. L. 107
Oliver 13, 15–6, 20, 24–5, 31–2, 35, 38–9, 44, 49, 52, 55, 57–8, 64, 78–80, f-80, 101–3, 107, 109, 112, 114, 119, 127, 160, 164, 176–8, 181, 198, 218, 247
Stephen 52, 176
William 53
W. W. 67
PHENIX
Robert 124
PHETTEPLACE
Randall 192
PHILBRICK
Herbert 267

PHILIPPE
    William 157
    Thomas 144
PHILIPS
    Jenks 146
    Jonathan 147
    John 143
    Peter 162
    Philo 221–2
PHILLIP 91, 156, 258
PHILLIPPS
    John 174
    Lorenzo 156
PHILLIPS 229
    Abeather 258
    Alva 245
    Ambrose 60
    B. 240
    Curtis 174
    Cyrene 235
    D. M. 240
    Daniel 228
    David 257
    Eliza 242
    Elizabeth 235
    George 245
    Hannah 242
    Isaac 154, 219
    John 156, 235, 240, 254, 259
    Jonathan 242
    Joshua 54, f-227, 230, 232, 235, 242
    Luther 240–2
    Mary 235
    Melvin 245
    & Montgomery 155
    Olive 235
    Peter 186
    Philo 90
    Pitts 230
    Priscilla 242
    Richard 245
    Sarah 235
    Thomas 157
    William 113, 141, 235
PHINNEY
    Harvey 167
PHIPP
    Luke 205
PHIPPS
    David 186, 195
    S. 257
PHOENIX BLOCK 105
PIATT
    Peter 205
PICKER
    Patrick 123
PICKERING
    Timothy 22–3
PICKET
    David 154
PICKETT 91
    David 49, 52
    S. D. 232
PIERCE 105
    Annie 66
    Byron 121
    Charles 174
    Ellis 141
    Ezra 52–3, 176
    Franklin 223, 250
    Henry 105
    J. A. 249
    Jackson 141
    John 156

PIERCE (cont.)
    Jonathan 264
    Kellogg 174
    Lucius 53
    Morse & Antis 105
    Nathan 18, 176–8, 180–1, 193
    Otis 264
    Phineas 129, 148
    Polly 181
    Reuben 217
    Rufus 180
    S. 108
    W. G. 229
    William 141, 174
PIERPONT 232
    Carolyn 235
    D. A. 227, 232
    David f-54, 227, 232, 235
    Frances 235
    H. B. 232, 242
    Ogden 235
    Sally Palmer 235
    Sarah Phillips 235
    Warren 232
PIERPONT'S TAVERN 231
PIERRON 33
PIERSALL 266
PIERSON 92, 155
    Edward 108
    Henry 200
    Job 204
    & Parrish 105
    R. H. 105
    Reuben 174
    Richard 80
PIKE
    Jeremiah 141
    Thomas 116
    William 141
PILLSBURY
    D. 217
    Henry 223
    M. 217
    May 221
    W. D. 218
    William 218, 221
PINCH
    John 108
    William 141
PINDAR 266
PINKERTON
    Jno. 124
PINKEY
    J. 150
PINKNEY
    Chas. 167, 169
    T. A. 167
    Theodore 169
PIPER 15
PITKIN
    C. J. 168
    Charles 174
PITKINS
    Chester 163
PITT 24, 54
    William 148
PITTS 11, 26, 33
    Abigail 231
    Benton 229
    Cyrus 232, 258
    George 232
    Gideon 17, 41, 49, 52, 106, 114, 225, 228–31
    Hannah 227

PITTS (cont.)
    Hiram 49, 228, 257
    Peter 17, 19, 36, 225, 227–8, 230–2, 236, 239
    Samuel 104, 225, 254–5
    Selah 241
    William 36, 225, 230, 239
PITT'S FLATS 254
PIXLEY
    Betsey 242
PLACE
    Amos 251
PLANTER
    J. S. 97
PLAT
    Ezra 63, 111
PLATNER 83–4
    John 84, 97, 144
PLATT 24, 38–9
    Eliphalet 242
    E. A. 220
    Ezra 34, 79
    Isaac 30
    S. H. 141
    Samford 90
    Starr 125
PLATTUM
    John 143
PLAYFORD
    James 173
    Stephen 173
PLEASANTON 87, 98
PLEASANTS 166
    C. S. 68
PLIMPTON
    Aaron 219
    Amasa 233
    William 222
PLIMTON PLACE 219
PLUM
    William 194
PLUMLEY
    Albert 156
PLUMMER
    Hiram 186
POAST
    Isaiah 263
POLAN
    Arthur 186
POLLAN
    James 157
POLLARD
    Edward 124
POLLEY
    Stanley 251
    Theodore 251
POLLOCK
    Robert 148
POLUM
    John 144
POMARNE
    Frederick 124
POMEROY 115
    Aaron 115, 181
    C. G. 115
    C. S. 161
    Calvin 211, 212
    M. S. 115
    Robert 56, 105
    Samuel 30
    Theodore 124
PONCETT
    Joseph 108

POND
    E. A. 258
    George 166
POOL 241
    J. F. 241, 243
    Mary 235
POOLE'S MILL 215
POOR
    Joseph 108
POPE 84, 96
    John 121
    Lydia 215
    Samuel 143
POPPINS
    Daniel 45
POPPLE
    B. G. 89
    William 180–1
PORTER 44, 86–7, 146, 149, 209
    Ambrose 169
    Augustus 13, 16–7, 20, 23, 29, 32–4, 38, 47–8, 52–3, 58, 102, 104, 111, 206, 209
    Desdemona 266
    Fitz-John 86
    John 266, 268
    Joseph 107
    Joshua 146, 206
    Josiah 52–3, 212
    Lansing 211
    Luther 159
    Marvin 57
    Moses 241
    Nathan 144
    Noah 40
    Orange 258
    P. B. 52
    Peter 26, 29, 32–3, 37–8, 45, 47, 53, 63, 79, 103, 116
    Robert 267
    Ruth 263, 265
    Stephen 148
    Sylvester 144, 174
    Thomas 266
    William 266
PORTER'S DIVISION 84, 86
POST 146, 208
    Abraham 52, 136
    Abram 49, 146
    Charles 146
    J. W. 166
    John 65, 78
    Jonathan 168
    Louisa 208
    Russell 66, 102
    William 182
POTTER 74, 100, 118, 105
    Arnold 78
    E. S. 116
    Hiram 53
    Horatio 74
    J. W. 116
    James 30, 108
    John f-78, 113
    Marvin 58
    Seth 201
    W. G. f-130
    Ziba 167
POTTLE
    E. B. 49
    Emory 52, 263
    Loring 264
POUND
    Charles 174
    Daniel 174

POUND (cont.)
    David 194
    Elijah 192
    Hugh 192, 194
    Isaac 174
    John 192
    Joseph 174
    Mary 195
    William 194–5
POWELL 24, 82-a, 106, 109, 128, 180
    A. V. H. 204
    Edith 82–b
    Edwin 106
    F. & Company 55
    Howell 169
    I. M. 82-a, 82-b
    James 82-a
    John 12, 203
    Martha 82-a
    Samuel 162
    Shotwell 52, 82-a, 264, 265
    T. J. 82-a
    Thomas 21, 129, 135, 143, 251
    William 55, 130, 182
POWELL'S 55
    Hotel 64, 128, 130
POWER
    Abiather 190
    Arthur 190, 194
    Melvin 190
    Moses 190, 193
    Orlin 196
    Robert 190, 220
    Waterman 190
POWERS
    Abiatha 193
    Abiather 193
    James 141
    John 263
    Robert 211
    Samuel 153
    Thomas 60
PRALT
    Robert 143
PRATT 103, 177–8, 191
    Augustus 177
    David 218
    Ebenezer 44, 177, 180
    Edwin 141
    Elim 157
    Elisha 152, 153, 225
    Elkanah 177
    Elvin 157
    Hannah 155
    Harry 211
    Hiram 173
    J. R. 108, 181, 184
    Jonathon 53
    Margaret 177
    Nathan 152
    Peter 193
PRENTICE
    David 74
PRESCOTT
    G. H. 166
    Imly 53, 136
    Joel 35, 168
    Messr. 67
PRESTER 166
PRESTON
    William 148
PRICE 116, 159
    Andrew 133
    Elizabeth 179

PRICE (cont.)
    Francis 186
    Henry 179
    Hiram 141
    Isaac 193
    John 38, 40, 49, 51–2, 159–60
    Sarah 179
    Thomas 120
PRICHARD
    G. C. f-164, 166
    George 173
PRINCE 65
    Frederick 53, 58, 77, 97
PRINDLE
    Henry 212
PRINGLE
    Benjamin 58
PRITCHARD
    Harrison 162
    Jabez 119
    Smith 119
PRITCHETT
    George 90, 141
PROBASCO
    Amasa 154, 174
    George 141
    Henry 143
    Lansing 143
    Rush 141, 143
    Uriah 141
PROCTOR 22
PROPER
    Dolly 43
PROUDFIT
    C. H. 131
    Charles 141, 148
PROUT
    George 122
PROUTY
    Ezra 156
    P. 77
    Phineas 58, 77–8, 129–30, 133, 136
    Steven 122
    William 119
PROVOST
    Augustine 111
    Louis 80
PRU
    Nathan 144
PRUYN
    A. B. 166
    H. B. 168
    M. 166
PRYOR
    Elisha 257
PULLEN
    Nicholas 164
PULTENEY 107
    Thomas 31
    William 247
PULTNEY
    William 20, 31–2, 127, 247
PULVER
    H. W. 256
    Henry 257
    J. M. 156
    Jas. 53
    William 155
PURCELL
    I. S. 228
    Isaac 53
    Orrin 234
PURDY 159
    J. 116

PURDY (cont.)
Jonathan 186
PURINGTON
W. F. 266
PURINTON
Thomas 167
PURLEE
Wilbur 234
PURSEL
Almira 258
Benjamin 256
Daniel 258
Edmund 258
John 258
Orra 259
Peter 256
William 256
PUTNAM 124
Charles 204
Levi 124
Victor 259
Willis 195
PUTS
Hiram 157

Q

QUACKENBUSH
Abram 245
QUAYLE
Charles 226
QUEAL
William 242
QUICK 228
J. A. 229
J. A. & Co. f-140
Jonas 257–9
Miles 124
Selah 120
QUIGLEY
William 186
QUINN
Esther 30, 212
Michael 186
Thomas 141

R

RADCLIFF
James 130
RAFTER
George 168
Lafayette 174
RAGH
Thomas 124
RAIFNES
J. 113, 132
John 88, 109, 113, 221
Thomas 58
William 243
RALPH
John 203
RAMISH
William 196
RAMSDELL
G. 49
Jonathan 194
RAMSEUR 99
RMASEY
A. F. 168
Charles 144
D. 168

RAND
Samuel 58
RANDALL
Almond 251
Edward 162
Ephraim 251
G. S. 248
Gaius 248, 251
George 204
James 213
N. W. f-98, 238, 240, 243
Norman 238
Stetson 120
William 162
RANDOLPH
G. 127
John 102
RANKINE 75, 130, 132
James 75, 80, 82
John 49, 80
RANNEY
Isac 213
Robert 259–60
RANSFORD 206
Archibald 206, 207
RANSOM
Asa 127
Millard 195
William 17
RANSON
Asa 127
RANSTED
Lewis 113
RAPPALEE 153
RAPPAL
Eugene 213
RASS
Charles 141
RAWLEIGH
Samuel 169
RAWSOME
A. 127
RAWSON
A. P. 199
Andrew 251
Lydia 203
M. L. 110
Maria 203
Porter 199
Samuel 49, 52, 199, 202
RAY 166, 228, 256–7
A. L. 141
Elizabeth 236
Ellen 236
George 227
Henry 52
John 236, 257
Mark 236
O. F. 256
Oscar 254
Peter 186
Wesley 234
RAYMOND
Charles 124, 174
Daniel 194
Ebenezer 204, 242
George 267
H. 141
Lucy 168
RAYNER
Peter 168
READ 35, 165
Seth 35, 165
Wheeler 230

RECORD
D. B. 177
RED JACKET 12–3, 15, 22–6, 39, 127
REDDOUT
W. N. 115
REDFIELD
Charles 182
Daniel 262
George 90, 174, 181, 195
Harley 178, 180
Hemen 177, 180
Lewis 66, 177
Lysander 168
Manning 177, 180–1
Margaret 161
Mary 177
N. 189
Orrin 165
Peleg 18, 24, 28, 177, 180
Spencer 186
W. H. C. 177
W. W. 68
REDMOND
Elizabeth 179
REECE 44
REED 25, 127, 129, 145–7, 248
Abner 242, 240
Adelia 237
Alanson 242, 245
Almeron 233, 237
Amanda 178
Amelia 237
Antha 237
Artemus 161
Asa 177
Augustus 240
Calvin 177
Chester 262
Cynthia 236
Daniel 89, 186, 242
Dustin 145
Elmira 235
Emily 237
Ezekiel 240
Fannie 2366
Frank 105
G. W. 209
George 53, 239, 241–2
H. H. 228
Hamson 186
Harmon 237
Isaac 186
Israel 118, 208
Jacob 12, 16, 146–7
James 108, 239, 246
John 70, 74, 103, 115, 148, 225, 231, 236–7
Jonathan 147, 190
Joshua 240
Louisa 237
Lovina 242
M. B. 264
Mason 152
Melancthon 147
N. A. 147
Nathan 40, 136
Nelson 144
Newton 146
Norman 237
Orrin 178
P. 231
Phila 35, f-227
Philiaa 237
Philipp 19, 225, 227–8, 230–1, 237

REED (cont.)
Rebekah 231
& Rockwood 105
Sally 246
Samuel 152, 154
Seth 12, 18, 20, 127, 144, 198
Seymour 241
Silas 152, 154, 225
T. R. 231
Talcott 118
Thomas 22, 186, 228, 235, 255
W. A. 159
Walter 237
Wheeler 225, f-227, 230, 237
William 122, 124, 162, 225
Wilson 146
REED'S MILL f-80
REES
James 51, 53, 58, 69, 72-3, 130
Margaret 167
REESE 129
James 22, 127-9, 135-6
Solomon 174
William 203, 242
REEVES 32, 33 104
James 116
John 257
Theophilus 205
William 123
REGNELL
James 144
REID
Charles 233
REILEY
Lawrence 156, 169
REINHART 169
REMER
Aaron 52
Isaac 163
John 123, 268
REMINGTON 118
Emery 59
S. W. 136
Thaddeus 117-8, 180
& Williams 59
REMY 257
John 257
RENWICK
Jane 119
REQUA 266
REW
Chloe 211
Ephraim 206-7, 211
Lot 111, 206, 208-9, 219
REYNOLDS 147
C. C. 161
H. E. 147
Hiram 223
J. B. 141
James 135
John 174
Peter 158
Silas 251, 254-9
Thomas 254, 257
REZNOR
John 108
Lot 123
RHODES
John 225, 229-30, 250
Jonathan 225
W. L. 108
RIALL 44
RICE 156, 247-9, 259
Aaron 40, 241, 248-9

RICE (cont.)
Caleb 168, 169
& Carpenter 166
Charles 147, 149, 174
Daniel 49, 207
Edward 146
Frank 53, 147
George 53, 207, 212
H. J. 146, 148
Jacob 176
James 147, 148
Jane 147
Levi 230
Lydia 169
Myron 176
O. F. 156
Oliver 35
T. D. 207
William 213
RICHARDS 76, 218
Benjamin 76
C. F. 255
Ezra 251
Floyd 258
& Norton 104
William 251
RICHARDSON 25, 131, 132
Amasa 259
C. 254
C. C. 136
Charles 53, 90, 121
Chester 257
E. B. 132
Edward 132
F. E. 133
George 259, 260
Gould 201
Jeremiah 201
John 19, 255
Jonathan 259
& Nichols 50
Paul 191, 200
Samuel 202
Sellick 201, 202
Silas 201
William 58, 255-7, 266
RICHIE
Isaac 144
RICHMOND
David 202
Deborah 225
H. 111
& Miller 106
Phoebe 220
Robert 220
RICKENSON
Benjamin 189
RICKER
John 159
RICKERSON
Benjamin 192
RIDDLE 44
John 191
Robert 191
RIDER
Benson 161
George 111
Jarvis 194
RIDLEY
Thomas 174
W. W. 115
RIFFORD
Frederick 107
& Wagstaff 114

RIGDON
Sydney 42
RIGGS
Solomon 120
RILANDS 147
Leonard 145
RILEY 200
Barnet 124
Daniel 219
David 186
George 157
John 186
Joseph 157
RINGER
Alonzo 141
Charles 144
David 146
Jacob 146
John 146
RINGER FAMILY 146
RIPLEY 45
RIPPEY 147
A. C. 147
Aaron 147
Addison 147
George 147
Hamilton 147
J. Grove 147
J. N. 147
James 147
John 147, 149
Martha 146
Mathew 146, 147
Robert 147
Thomas 146-7, 149
William 146
RIPPLE
Jackson 158
RISDEN
Daniel 231
Elijah 230
Moses 228
O. 225
Oresimus 226
RISON
Wallace 157
RISS
Joseph 141
RISSER
Abraham 116
Henry 116
James 116
RITTENHOUSE
David 20
RITTER
Edward 223
Frederick 141
RIVERS
John 122
RIX
Clark 258
Lewis 258
ROACH 84
ROAD
Alex 124
ROBB
William 128
ROBBINS
J. G. 191
James 86
ROBERSON
Benjamin 40
ROBERT
J. T. 169

ROBERT (cont.)
  N. L. 110
ROBERTS 170, 209
  Abraham 248
  Amasiah 124
  Anna 169
  George 174
  Henry 174
  Israel 113
  James 174
  Joel 40
  Moses 108
  Orin 243
  Palmer 141, 169
  William 158
ROBERTSON
  Charles 109
  J. L. 133
  Robert 144
ROBESON
  Fanny 195
  Jane 155
  John 163
ROBINETT
  James 214
ROBINS
  Charles 35
ROBINSON 22, 24, 34, 101, 147, 154, 206
  Andrew 174
  B. 258
  Benedict 15, 49, 128
  Charles 112, 113, 186
  Daniel 52, 194
  Dennison 261
  Edwin 174, 186
  Frederick 234
  Gain 63, 66
  H. N. 81
  Harry 181
  Henry 35
  Horatio 80
  J. 257
  James 155, 174
  John 17-8, 101, 120, 180, 186, 221
  Joseph 147
  Mary 30
  Robert 166
  Thomas 261
  Wesley 157
  William 158
ROBINSON'S FOUNDRY 103
ROBISON 164
  Andrew f-172
  Anna f-172
  Catharine f-172
  Charles 174
  Edna f-172
  James 164, f-172
  Harry 164, f-172
  Jane f-172
  John 164, 167, 170, f-172
  Luther f-172
  Mahala f-172
  S. D. 77
  Sarah f-172
  William 174
ROBSON
  John 144, 147
  Phebe f-154
  S. 147
  William f-154
ROCHESTER
  John 44
  Nathaniel 39, 52

ROCHESTER (cont.)
  Thomas 80
ROCKAFELLOW 257
  Norman 168
ROCKWELL 43, 118
  J. L. 108
  James 123
ROCKWOOD
  John 105
  Lewis 123
  & Reed 105
RODGERS
  David 123
RODNEY
  Cornelius 141
  John 186
  Theodore 120, 186
ROE
  A. C. 133
  John 233
  Peter 144
  Robert 186
  William 168, f-172, 188
ROGERS 135, 146
  Aaron 144
  Albert 186
  Alexander 211
  C. H 179
  H. B. f-92
  James 206
  John 53
  Joseph 105
  Lewis 211
  Melbury 141
  Oscar 121, 245
  Samuel 114, 135
  Sarepta 169
  Thomas 45
  William 52, 178
ROHR
  Gottlieb 205
  Rudolph 205
ROLLINSON
  William 205
ROLPH
  John 32, 34, 61, 111, 250
ROMEYN 134
  James 134
ROOD
  Daniel 242
  Jonathan 255
  Sally 242
ROOT 83, 106, 132, 168, 229
  A. Langdon 133
  Abigail 255
  Abraham 112, 118
  Asa 201, 202
  Augustus 168, 174
  C. 108
  Catherine 188
  Chauncy 124
  Desire 176-7
  Edward 159
  Esquire 60
  F. 167
  Francis 165-6, 168
  G. W. 133
  George 132
  Henry 205
  Hezekiah 113
  Isaac 199, 202-4
  James 167
  John 159
  Luther 165-6

ROOT (cont.)
  R. 60
  Rosewell 113, 118
  Roswell 113
  Rowland 159
ROPER
  John 251
ROPP
  John 157
ROSE 19, 135, 180, 210
  Anna 209, 211
  Arthur 78
  David 205
  Elijah 117, 198, 211
  Elisha 209
  George 186
  Irving 205
  Jarius 114, 117
  Jennette 203
  John 60, 200, 202-3
  Justus 117, 119
  Lansing 266
  Oliver 104, 117, 119
  P. H. 103, 105
  R. L. 227
  Robert 52, 135, 156, 235
  Sherman 132
  Washington 205
ROSEBURGH
  James 52
ROSECRANS 91
ROSEMAN
  Palmer 258
ROSS, 166
  Albert 144
  & Cooley 166
  Daniel 259
  David 251
  George 186
  Peter 259
  Smith 251
  William 144, 254
ROSSER 99
ROSSITER 84
ROTH
  J. W. 231
ROTHEAR
  Henry 234
ROULETTE 264
ROUP
  William 199
ROUSE
  Henry 186
  William 122
ROWE
  Cornelia 203
  E. 37
  Erastus 210
  George 204
  James 141
  John 124, 223
  William 56, 168, 181
ROWELL
  Sheppard 268
ROWLAND
  Nerian 124
ROWLATT
  William 155
ROWLEY 207
  A. H. 210
  Charles 205
  Frank 200, 213
  Franklin 124
  J. 203

Index of Names to the 1876 History of Ontario County, New York

ROWLEY (cont.)
Jirah 200–2
John 119
Joseph 201, 202
Lendall 259
Levi 118, 119
Lucy 212
Nelson 174
Rebecca 119
Richard 214
S. 210
Simeon 210, 212
W. J. 201
ROWLEY'S SCHOOLHOUSE 119
ROY
Coll 165
George 259, 260
Isaac f-171
John 168
Thomas 165
ROYAL
Nelson 162
William 162
ROYCE
Oliver 176, 181
Robert 53, 67, 110
RUPERG
John 174
RUBERTS
Alanson 174
Alfred 174
John 174
RUDD
Darwin 141
John 74
RUES
Ephraim 18
Lot 18
RUFF
Eliza 113
RUGAR
D. H. 108
RUGGLES 129
RUMNEY
John 136
Robert 136
RUMSEY 55, 218
John 58, 180
RUNNER
W. A. 156
RUNYAN 156
C. A. 109
Henry 186
Samuel 158
RUPELL
Francis 169
RUPERT
William 149
RUPP
D. C. M. 108
RUPRECHT
John 141
RUSH 178
D. 193
Mary 178
R. M. 193
Rhoda 178
Russell 36, 49, 178, 180
Samuel 178, 180, 193
RUSHMORE
Jeremiah 181
RUSSEL
Carlos 144

RUSSELL
Allen 152
Benjamin 17, 189
Catharine 168
Charles 152
Enoch 168
George 141
John 159, 186
R. 149
Robert 186
RUTHERFORD 259
RYAN
J. A. 248
James 179
John 222, 248
Joseph 109, 152
Timothy 181
William 121, 213
RYCKMAN 127
Peter 12, 16, 20, 127

S

SABIN 258
B. 169
Benjamin 169, 203
Hiram 263
P. D. 166
Philo 168
Zadoc 267
SACKET
Zelotus 264
SACKETT 116, 153, 202
Angus 117
Arze 125
Augustine f-72, 116–7, 125
D. C. 112
Darius 125, 121
F. A. f-116
Fosket & Carter 118
George 50, 124
Homer 125
Sarah 125
Samuel 144
Theron 116, 125
SADDLER
Ebenezer 219
SADLER
L. L. 136, 203
SAGE
George 213
Giles 178
J. R. 243
James 214
Lydia 178
O. N. 113
Orson 178
Oscar 213
Ranson 207, 221
SAGERTY
James 124
SAILOR 249
ST. CLAIR 22
ST. CROIX
Louis 172
ST. JOHN 44
George 231
Myron 185
ST. JOHNS 262
SALES
Leonard 204
SALISBURY 168
Amasa 119

SALISBURY (cont.)
B. F. f-174
Hezekiah 66
John 164, 166
Joseph f-90
S. W. 38
Samuel 108
Smith 66
William 168
SALMON
John 253
Richard 70, 74
Stephen 207, 212
SALRAN
Henry 144
SALSBURY
Harrison 249
Samuel 53
SALTER
Hugh 254
John 214
Thomas 214
SALTONSTALL 29, 103, 109
Dudley 32, 47, 52–3, 63, 78–9, 112
SAMMONS 90
SAMPSON
Aleck 153
SANBORN 29, 101–3
Hannah 23
Nathaniel 17, 33–4, 78–9, 101–2, 111, 164, f-172
P. F. 220
SANBORN'S TAVERN 102
SANBURN 47
SANDERS
John 124
SANDERSON
Cynthia 169
David 169
George 136
SANFORD
Charles 251
Daniel 122
Edgar 120
Henry 123
J. M. 249
M. S. 58, 132
Philip 242
SANGER
H. K. 58, 111
Henry 53
Jedediah 14, 115
SANGER PLACE 178
SARDUN
Samuel 144
SARGENT & HUGHES 201
SATTER
Hugh 256
SAUL
George 124
Robert 108
SAULISBURY
Samuel 161
SAULPAUGH
John 142
Philip 144
SAULSPAUGH
Philip 174
SAUNDERS
Elias 144
Elizabeth 152
Eunice 40
Harvey 115
Joseph 24

SAUNDERS (cont.)
   Robert 115
SAUNDERSON
   David 166
SAVAGE
   Edward 142
   John 227
SAVILL
   Joseph 228
SAWTELLE
   Levi 155
   Mason 155
   Sarah 155
SAWYER 36, 38
   Augustus 52, 161
   Desire 177
   E. 38
   Edward 41
   Hooker 176-7, 180
   J. M. 38
   Joseph 177, 182
   Norris 178
   Schuyler 176
   Thomas 176, 180, 256
SAXBY PLACE 208
SAXE
   Asa 182
SAXTON 106
   Asher 208, 211-2
   DeWitt 142
   Frederick 13, 17, 101
   Philander 208, 212
   Stephen 53, 106
SAXTON LOT 109
SAYLES
   Hiram 263
   Stephen 263, 265
SAYLOR
   Eliphalet 54
SAYRE
   C. H. 58
   Cooper 50, 168
   J. 129
   J. B. 258
SAYTON
   William 144
SCANTLIN
   Jno. 124
   W. 115
SCANTLING
   Daniel 121
   Michael 120, 123, 186
   Oliver 186
SCHELLINGER
   William 124
SCHEMERHORN
   Abraham 57
SCHERLE
   Charles 142
SCHERMERHORN
   Norton 144
   J. M. 109
   S. V. R. 142
SCHICK
   George 186
SCHOFIELD 89
SCHOLTZ
   Jno. 121
SCHOON
   John 147
SCHRODER
   Frank 123
SCHULARS
   William 115

SCHURRLIFF
   A. H. 212
SCHUTT
   A. D. 158
   H. 93
   Hiram 186
   John 181
   Martin 174
SCHUYLER 156
   Peter 12
SCOFIELD
   C. W. 142
SCOON
   John 130, 133
SCOT
   Albert 69
   Robert 69
SCOTT 45, 91, 167
   Adonijah 174
   Augustus 142
   Brian 142
   Charles 163
   Cornelius 196
   David 174
   Elwood 194
   Ferris 167
   Henry 144
   James 186
   John 143, 233
   Lewis 121
   Myron 144
   Reuben 142
   Robert 128, 136
   Sally 169
   William 58, 143
SCOVIL
   Hiram 169
SCOVILL
   Abijah 227
   Michael 227
SCOVILLE
   Ezra 169
SCRAMLING
   A. 200
SCRANTON
   Edwin 25
   Hamlet 108
SCUDDER
   Ezekiel 18, 200, 202
   Jesse 202
SCULL
   Joseph 33, 203
SCULLEN
   Joseph 186
SEABURY
   E. Morgan 174
SEAGER 221
   Darwin 182
   Edwin 170
   Franklin 170
   Levi 170
   Micah 221
SEAMAN
   Christian 119
SEAMANS
   F. 249
   H. G. 158
   Isaac 90, 267
   William 267
SEARBURY
   George 144
   John 144
SEARLES
   George 266

SEARS 147
   Abigail 240
   Alanson 210
   Alden 18, 240-1
   Charles 186
   Clinton 170
   D. C. 240
   David 242
   Delano 242
   J. P. 19
   J. S. 132
   J. Sanford 133
   James 132, 149
   Jasper 212, 216-7
   John 113, 241
   S. B. 210
SEAVERY
   William 203
SEBRAN
   Hiram 124
SECOR
   Joseph 256
   T. J. 174
SEDGWICK 85, 92
   A. G. 142
   Theodore 177
SEELEY
   Benjamin 222
   James 257
   Seymour 144
SELLYE
   Frank 156
   Hiram 132
   Isaac 132
SEEMNER
   John 158
SEIGLAR
   Charles 174
SEIGWALT
   Jacvob 174
SEITZ
   Leonard 142
SELBY
   Ira 52
SELDON
   Marion 80
SELEY
   Mary 113
SELLAGE
   James 158
SELLMAN
   Thomas 109
SELLON
   John 111
   O. P. 266
SELMSER 130
SELOVER 132
SENNATTE
   Wm. 120
SENNOTT
   William 124
SERGEANT
   Isaac 256, 258
SERRIGAN
   John 157
SERVICE
   Jas. 108
SEUEL
   George 142
SEVERANCE 257
   A. 255-7
   Artemus 255, 257
   Charles 174, 182
   H. C. 166

SEVERANCE (cont.)
Henry 174
T. C. 166
SEVOY
Lewis 123
SEWARD
Frederick 54
Isaac 229, 251
James 181
SEXTON 116
Joseph 116
SEYMOUR 110, 228
Belden 204
Charles 57, 111, 263
H. 64
Henry 213
Ira 199, 202–3
Isaac 58
J. 219
James 57
Johnson 203
Joseph 204
L. 111, 116
O. 111
Robert 144
Stephen 179
Z. 56
Zacaruah 263
Zachariah 44, 103, 111, 116, 118, 178, 263
SHA
Anson 113
SHABOLT
Darius 150
Martha 150
Sarah 150
SHADDOCK
Benjamin 223
George 224
Henry 223
Searmus 224
SHAFER, D. & CO. 105
SHAFFER
Harris 196
Peter 40
SHANK 256
John 257
SHANNON
John 53
SHARP 206
Peter 202
SHARPSHINS 16
SHARPSTEEN
George 231
SHARPSTEIN
George 228
SHATTOCK
Albert 223
SHAW 166
Abijah 263
Edward 166, 180
Eli 258
George 142, 166
Gideon 199
Hannah 113
Isaac 153
John 166, 180
Samuel 263
Thomas 166, 180
Washington 67
SHAY 169, 176
Anson 160
Asa 160
John 245

SHEAR
Henry 174
SHEARMAN
Jacob 142
SHEARS
Charles 205
Theodore 186
SHECKEL
Samuel 135
SHECKELL
Clara 160
Cornelia 160
Hattie 160
Henry 160
R. H. 160, 181
SHEEHAN
Jno. 213
SHEEP
Aleck 153
SHEFFER
Ceylon 186
H. C. 180
Mary 182
Roswell 182
SHEFFIELD
Catharine 169
John 192
SHEKELL 178
Benjamin 178, 181
C. 73
John 178, 180, 182
Nancy 178
Richard 160, 178, 181
SHELDON 40, 250
Benjamin 117, 126
Deacon 201
G. C. 108
Gardner f-196
George 124, 222
James 129, 186
Joseph 192
Levi 186
Minerva 126
Orimel 117
Submit 227
W. H. 218
Wareham 30
William 223
SHELDON TAVERN STAND 118
SHELTON
Frederick 224
Joseph 52
William 223, 234
SHEPARD 153
A. G. 255
Augustus 253
C. E. 50, 115
Chas. 49
Charles 53, 111, 115
Edward 80
George 220, 231
Horace 259
J. F. 217
James 80
M. F. 49
Nathaniel 202, 216
Willard 259
William 44–5, 53, 63, 107, 112, 259
SHEPARD'S POND 217
SHEPHARD 216
Charles 195
T. 38
John 162
Theodore 79

SHERIDAN 82, 92, 94, 97–9
William 109
SHERMAN 88, 92, 98, 154, 218–9
Ab. E. 142
E. W. f-170
John 104, 164
Levi 251
Robert 31
Watts 28
SHERRED 70
SHERRILL 91
E. 90, 142
SHERWOOD 152
George 144
John 55
S. A. 108
SHETHAR
John 129
SHETTERS
David 205
SHIEBLY 129
SHIELDS
Fanny 169
Truston 169
William 124
SHIMEALL
Richard 111
SHIMER 91
Isaac 90
SHIMMER
Isaac 142
SHIPPEX
John 157
SHIRLEY
John 24, 245
SHIVER
John 158
SHOEMAKER
Joseph 119
SHOLES
David 144, 174
Fifield 174
Henry 174
William 174
SHOOK
John 130
SHORT 166
Abel 228
Daniel 228, 234
David 57
Enos 174
H. 228
James 174
John 174
Leonard 181
Philip 227–8, 230, 235
Ralph 174, 186
S. D. 234
Seneca 255
S. Truman 255
T. 56, 59
Theophilus 59, 178–80, 239
William 176–7, 228
SHORT'S FLATS 253
SHORTSLIVES 96
SHOTTS
Adam 144
SHOTWELL 190
SHROPE
Samuel 118
SHULARS
John 115
SHULTERS
Henry 161

SHULTS
    J. E. 142
    John 162
SHURTLIFF
    Alonzo 212, 232
    George 123
SHUTE
    Henry 168
SHUTT
    Hiram 52, 53
SIBBART
    John 263
SIBBETTS
    Walter 186
SIBLEY 24, 38, 107, 221
    Eber 225
    Edgar 124
    Elijah 230
    James 104, 108, 110, 232
    M. H. 57, 107
    Mark 39, 41, 49, 51–2, 56, 76, 104, 111
    O. E. 108
    William 226
SICKLES 91
SID WAY
    C. 207
SIDWAY
    J. J. 105
SIEBERT
    Charles 99
SIEGMUND
    George 76
SIGEL 97
SIGLER
    Charles 142
    James 142
    William 144
SILVERNAIL
    William 210
SILL
    William 58
SILSBY 218
SIMMONS 109, 113, 241
    Abigail 242
    Alanson 110
    Albert f-74
    Asa 225
    B. S. 210
    Benjamin 240–2
    Charles 245
    Constance 240
    Constant 241
    David 240
    E. W. 93
    Elnathan 52–3, 80
    Ephraim 240
    Frank 119
    Gamaliel 242
    George 245
    H. P. 241
    Harvey 205
    Henry 233, 241
    Isaac 201, 204
    Israel 202
    J. H. 116
    John 144, 240–1, 257
    Lydia 242
    Maria 246
    Matilaa 242
    Philip 241
    R. 243
    Richard 246
    Richmond 240, 243
    Robert 53, 242

SIMMONS (cont.)
    Sardis f-221
    Seth 239
    Simeon 240, 242
    Simon 211
    W. S. 243
    William 186
SIMMONDS
    Richmond 53
SIMONDS, A. & CO. 199
SIMONS
    Asa 17
    Benjamin 266
    Henry 267
    Jeremiah 219
    Levi 257
    William 259
SIMPSON 181
    Alexander 205
    Andrew 204
    James 122
    M. R. 141
    Robert 132, 218
    Sylvester 214
SINCLAIR 146
SINCLARE
    Foster 147
SINGER
    John 130
SINGLANT
    Henry 124
SINGLER
    Charles 186
SINGLETON
    Edward 123
SIHON 129
SISSON 132, 258
    Daniel 241, 245
    Horace 243, 245
    James 245
    John 242
    O. F. 239, 254
    Stephen 18, 120, 148, 241
    Thomas 35, 129, 165, 248
    William 245
SITTING BULL 98
SIZER
    Edward 204
SKAATS
    Daniel 130
SKEELE
    J. P. 211
SKEKELL
    Samual 182
SKERRITT
    Samuel 104
SKILTON & CO. 129
SKINNER 13, 159, 229–30
    Charles 203
    Jonas 257
    Nelson 228
    Sally 242
SLACY
    Edwin 179
SLAUSON
    P. S. 161, 195
SLAVES
    Phoebe 54 (Spencer)
    Sally 54 (Clark)
    Sylvia 54 (Spencer)
    Vin 54 (Atwater)
    William 54 (Atwater)
    Judith 53 (Saltonstall)
    Moody, Lindy 53 (Ferguson)

SLAVES (cont.)
    Lucy 178 (Shekell)
    Rose 178 (Shekell)
SLEGHT
    A. 227
SLENGERLARD 105
SLIGHT
    Mortimer 234
SLINGERLAND
    Henry 258
SLOAN
    J. 133
SLOAT
    John 157
    S. A. 110
SLOCUM 84
    Henry 82
SLOSSON
    B. 53
SLOUT 256, 257, 259
    Wesley 233
SLY 159
    Evander 105, 160
SMALLEY
    William 86
SMEDLEY 119
    James 44, 101, 106–7, 109, 177, 247
SMITH 18, 25, 42–3, 76–7, 83–4, 127, 156, 181,
    192–3, 201, 209, 218, 232, 258
    A. S. 166
    A. E. 117
    Abram 167
    Albert 117
    Alvah 42
    Arabella 76
    Asa 49, 194
    Augustus 124
    Baldy 93, 94
    Barclay 158
    Benjamin 118, 251, 268
    & Bradley 179
    Burton 245
    C. W. 124
    Caleb 228
    Catharine f-172
    Charles 110, 122, 144, 163, 218, 223
    Chauncey 124
    Chester 142, 163
    Clarence 269
    Syrenus 268
    D. G. 108
    Daniel 174, 186, 218, 230, 240
    David 40, 148, 174, 191, 193
    Dennis 233
    Dennison 156, 169
    E. 57
    E. A. 124
    E. K. 109
    Edgar 205
    Edson 174
    Edward 50, 131
    Elam 159
    Eldrick 218
    Elijah 35
    Elwood 192
    Ezra 258
    E. Fitch 52
    Francis 218
    Frederick 224
    Gazila f-172
    George 144, 174, 177, 193, 213, 218, 245,
    268
    Gerrit 199
    H. 227

SMITH (cont.)
H. M. 115
Hamilton 76
Harry 232
Henry 30, 61, 144, 228
Herman 222
Homer 259
Hugh 233
Ichabod 174
Isaac 63, 143
Isaiah 257, 259
J. W. f-130
Jacob 18, 190–1, 193, 216, 218
James 15, 51, 107, 142, 186, 218, 223, 233
Jared 190, 191
Jeremiah 251
Job 17, 129
John 33, 61, 78, 124, 174, 186, 157, 163, 205, 225, 230, 238–9, 241
Jonathan 19, 49, 59, 190, 193, 201–2, f-208, 211
Joseph 17, 19, 22, 42, 101–2, 179, 190–1, 193, 201–2, 258
Leonard 147
Levi 25, 190
Lindley 49
L. M. 109
Lucas f-162
Lucinda 177
L. W. 220
Lydia 190
M. 228
M. H. 133
Mc Loud, Snow & Hotchkiss 166
Mark 108
Mansel 254
Maurel 259, 260
Nathan 154
Nathaniel 49
Nicholas 198, 202, 212
Noah 192
O. H. 64, 109
O. L. 268
O. M. 113
Orasmus 70, 74
P. A. 190
P. S. 240
Perry 124
Peter 49, 191, 199
R. P. 191
Reuben 122, 191, 208
Richard 15, 25, 62
Robert 142, 257, 259
Roswell 123
Rufus 147
S. E. 132
S. W. 53
Samuel 233, 259
Seymour 89, 222, 245–6, 266
Silas 161, 174, 186
Solomon 132
Stephen 189, 191, 193, 240
Sylvester 147
T. 129
T. & Co. 130
Thomas 50, 131, 135, 192
Truman 130
Uriah 174
W. 259
W. A. 170
W. N. 130
W. P. 228
W. T. 83
Welcome 193

SMITH (cont.)
William 40, 50, 52–3, 60, f-92, 131–2, 147–8, 174, 191, 227, 232–3, 254, 258–9, 186, 192
Wilmarth 49, 193
Winfield 108
SMITH'S DIVISION 83, 93
SMITH'S MILL 192, 218
SMYTH
T. 248
SNAPP
Jacob 259
SNEDIKER
Hugh 186
John 186
SNELL
M. J. 132
SNELLING
Henry 142
James 142
John 142
SNOOK 153
D. 257
George 186
Jordan 186
SNOW 165
J. R. 166
S. C. 67
William 169
SNYDER 166
& Anabel 179
Benjamin 257
Charles 205
Martin 205
Mary 155
Peter 257
Philip 257
William 157
SNYDER MILL 166
SODEN
Charles 174
James 174
Thomas 186
William 174
SOLES
Eliab 228
SOLOMON
John 174
SONIGEN
Henry 158
SOPER
William 124
SORTELL
Levi 154
SOULE
Benjamin 195
Mahala 195
Mahitabil 155
Matthews & Co. 201
SOUTHARD
Alvah 49
SOUTHERLAND
Castle 130
SOUTHWICK
Albert 124
SOUTHWORTH
C. 40
Samuel 58
SOVERHILL 77
James 77
SPAFFORD 103
H. Gates 128
SPANGLE 159, 180
Abram 162

SPANGLE (cont.)
George 180
Henry 160
W. M. 109
Zachariah 159
SPAULDING 15, 38, 41, 87, 128
Asa 42, 108, 110
Erastus 169
Frederick 154
Jno. 124
SPEAKER
Alvire 196
SPEAR 40, 160
Chauncey 182
George 180, 182
John 53, 168
Robert 181
SPEARS
Alonzo 142
Chauncey 159
SPECKER
G. 208
SPEEKER
Myan 180
SPEER 166
Margaret 177
SPEKIN
Peter 177
SPELMEN
Lydia 125
SPENCE
Gideon 233
SPENCER 24, 79, 111, 118, 255
A. 242
Aaron 118, 238, 248
Abijah 239, 241
Ambrose 38–9, 45, 80
Charles 143
Daniel f-235
E. 255
Elijah 52
Ezra 254, 257
G. O. 259
George 256
Henry 124
Horace 259
Ichabod 79
Ira 256, 258–9
J. C. 56
J. W. 255, 259
John 32, 39, 44, 51–4, 56, 58, 64, 73, 79, 80, 109, 111, 112, 177
Joseph 256
L. 259
Newell 124
Orra 259
Philip 80
Robert 102, 104, 110
S. B. 255
Samuel 19, 254, 256
Selecta f-235
Thomas 104
Urial 256, 258–9
William 35, 49, 52
SPENDLOVE
Ed 142
Philip 144
William 144
SPERRY
James 210
Moses 18, 210
SPICER 249
Jabez 204
Jehial 256, 258–9

SPICER (cont.)
Jeremiah 247, 249
SPIER
D. D. 129
Joseph 170
SPINKS
John 161
SPITZ 209
SPOONER 168
Amelia 167
SPOOR 161
Abraham 177–9
Brainard 174
Charles 174
Cornelius 174
Derrick 103
Martin 174
W. T. 130, 131
SPRAGUE
Asahel 208
Betsey 208
David 63
George 50
James 214
John 194
L. 108
L. S. 105
Minta 208
Paul 268
Philetus 63
R. 52
Reuben 122
Roger 38, 53, 114, 206–9, 212, 230
Silas 208
Thomas 208, 212
William 211
SPRAY
Frank 174
SPRENER
Aaron 113
SPRING
B. D. 208
Ebenezer 208
Frank 213
George 213
H. J. 219
William 214
SPRINGSTEAD
Jonathan 130
Theodore 267
W. 142
SPROUL 67
SPROWLES
P. 258
SPURN
Abram 168
SPURR
Ranson 208
SQUIER
Aden 147
Alfred 147
E. A. 148
Ed 142
J. C. 148
Jesse 147
M. A. 156
R. 146
Seba 146, 148
SQUIRES
E. A. 148
George 123
H. S. 108
Henry 122

SQUIERS
Amasa 116
STACEY
Abram 254
Alonzo 174
Sylvanus 254
STACY
Albert 186
Mary 168
O. M. 168
Theodore 186
Thomas 181
STAFFORD 176, 218
Horatio 186
Milton 204
Roswell 182
William 186
STAFFPRD
Samuel 209
STAINTON
William 142
STALL
B. 109
James 157
John 120
STANCHELL 206
STANCLIFF
Samuel 263
STANDICH
John 251
STANDISH 56
Elihu 251
Matthew 257
Thomas 249
STANLEY 129, 214
A. 56
Asa 56, 64, 106–7, 109, 111
Bell f-62
& Clark 104
D. W. 108
Daniel 237
Elmira 237
Erastus 107, 108
Eunice 237
George f-62
Hiram 237
John 237
Julia f-62
Lucas f-62
Luther f-226, 228, 237
Lydia f-226
Lydia 237
Margaret Nichol f-62
Marietta 237
Mary 237
Salma 230
Seth 52, f-62, 132, 147
STANLIFF 120
STANNARD
A. R. 108
G. 108
STANSELLS 30
STANTON
Henry 144
James 174
John 174
STANWOOD
Ralph 257
STAPLES
Andrew 161
STARK
Aiken 231, 258
Albert 156
Arthur 174

STARK (cont.)
Charles 156
George 157
STARKS
T. F. 107
STARLING
Samuel 212
STARR
Elisha 66
G. H. 89
STAUNTON
John 130, 141
STAVERLY
Jonathan 174
STEAD
Elizabeth 161
STEADMAN
Libbie 148
STEARNS 259
A. 50
Addison 153
George 53
Joel 169
John 155
Jonathan 153
Royal 152
STEBBINFIELD
William 142
STEBBINS 170
Charles 169
J. H. 133, 168
J. J. 64, 109
J. N. 59
STEDD
Ellett 124
Henry 124
STEEL
Antha 237
Harvey 112
Joel 17
STEELE 112, 203, 209
Allen 156
Edgar 88, 212
Edward 208
Elephalet 34
Elisha 40, 209
George 213
Harriet 212
Harvey 49, 117
J. S. 208
J. W. 207
Joel 49, 206, 209
Julius 211, 220
Linus 210
Marana 214
Nathaniel 207
Phoebe 112
R. M. 58
Roderick 225
William 178
STEPHENS
Charles 186, 195
Henry 196
Jesse 228
John 162
Porter 157
Samuel 186
STEPHENSON
Calvin 165
Chester 165
Daniel 122, 268
Dolphis 165, 166
Harvey 165
Henry 144, 186

STEPHENSON (cont.)
J. 38
James 165
Luther 165
Robert 254
Theodore 165
William 165
STERLING
Daniel 122
James 258
STETSALL
John 174
STETSON
A. A. 50
John 251
STEVANS
John 106
STEVENS 66, 83, 229, 254
Ami 231
E. K. 231
George 144
H. 108
Hannah 150
Hebry 255
Henry 148
J. A. 110
Jacob 49
James 186
Jeremiah 162
Jesse 228
John 52, 58, 66, 106, 111
Joseph 157
Joshua 180
J. V. B. 149
Katy 254
Levi 55, 135
Perry 124
Peter 163
Richard 56, 142
Simon 254
Theron 144
Porter 123, 157
Walter 228
Willard 254
William 186, 231
STEVENSON 79, 116
Dolphus 52
Isaac 254, 255
James 79, 108
Richard 116
Thos. 108
William 196
STEWARD
George 212
STEWART 119, 217, 232
Charles 52, 86, 174
Daniel 168
Donald 21
Eliza 168
Frederick 90
G. H. 92
George 155
James 180
Joseph 266
Nancy 168
Rachael 168
Samuel 155
Stephen 144
William 213, 224
STEWART'S INDEPENDENT
VOLUNTEERS 86
STIDD
Elliott 251
Henry 251

STIFF-ARMED
George 26
STILES 119
Albert 214
E. 263
Sanford 233
STILLMAN
B. 104
Bennett
Ellicott 259
James 259
STILLWELL 206, 209
Abijah 211
Benjamin 211
Roxy 211
STINY
John 143
STOCK
Edward 162
STOCKING & BULL 104
STOCKTON 169
STODDARD
A. 264
Colvin 43
E. 207
James 45
R. W. 69
Robert 69, 128, 135-6
Richard 128
W. 159
STODDART 228
STOKE(S) 156
STOKIE 147
J. 147
Sarah 147
STOKOE
& Koehler 155
W. E. f-152
& Wilson f-152, 155
STONE 75, 167
Asahel 37
Caroline 168
Ebenezer 200
Eli 113
Harvey 49, 152
Isaac 209
James 75
John 74, 75
Olive 198
Theodore 221
William 124
STORMS 168
Ajaph 169
Henry 142
STORY 266
Dinah 256
Samuel 256
Stephen 263
STOTENBERG & DILLINGHAM 166
STOUT
Aaron 56
David 199
J. B. 108
Jesse 232
Nancy 257
P. I. 231
Theodosia 203
Thomas 186
Wesley 259
Z. Barton 52
STOUT'S TAVERN 229
STOUGHTENBURG
George 162

STOUGHTON
John 104
STOUTENBURG
Abram 136
STOUTENBURGH
William 182
STOW
Joseph 69, 128
STOWE 67
A. M. 107, 112
Timothy 220, 242
STRAIGHT
Marry 113
William 113, 144
STRATTON 248
Jerusha 30
STRAUGHTEN 147
STREET
Joseph 143
Samuel 12
STREETER
Ebenezer 155
STRONG 148
C. 67
Charles 221
Dwight 158
Elisha 52, 104, 106
Henry 155, 169
Nancy 148
Wm. 169
STROUP
George 141
STRUBLE
Adam 258
Charles 259-60
George 258-9
Henry 234, 259
John 258-9
M. 254
Simeon 255
STRUBLE FARM 255
STRYKER
Manning 211
STUART 98
George 170
Jesse 258
William 178
STUBBS
George 223
STURDEVANT
Holmes 157
STURGES
Henry 221, 224
William 221, 224
STURTEVANT
Homer 175
STUTWELL
Isaac 124
STYKER 166
STULES
Amos 229
John 122
SUCH
Christopher 268
Thomas 266
SULLIVAN 9, 11-3, 15-7, 127, 145, 164, 216,
229, 253, 256
Catharine 256
Gideon 256
John 143, 157, 213
Joseph 233
Martin 222
Michael 223
Solomon 245

SULLIVAN (cont.)
  William 256, 259, 263
SULLIVAN'S RAIDERS 247
SUMMERBELL
  S. N. 266
SUPPLEE
  C. Y. 105
  Charles 122
SUTHERLAND 58, 258
  A. S. 117
  Daniel 147
  David 40, 49, 51-2
  G. W. 147
  Jacob 51
  John 117, 180, 182
  Morris 160
  Reuben 117, 159
  Thompson 117
  William 117
SUTPHEN 110
  Gilbert 53, 109
SUTTON 239
  Abraham 263, 265
  Betsey 266
  Calvin 263
  Charles 83
  Elisha 263
  George 268
  Isaac 263
  Jacob 264
  Jemima 266
  John 263
  Judith 266
  S. H. 263-5
  Seymour 264
  William 130
SUTTON'S SETTLEMENT 250
SUYDHAM
  W. H. 130
  William 130
SWALLOW
  A. J. 131
  J. 161
SWAN 230
  A. 170
  Alonzo 168
  Amos 255
  Cyrus 254
  Edward 174
  George 225
  H. C. 56
  John 133
  M. 168
  R. J. 132
  Robert 58, 132
  Seneca 255
SWART
  Jeremiah 152
SWARTHOUT
  Benj. 108
  James 124
SWARTOUT 14
SWARTS
  Daniel 255
  Peter 258
SWARTS FARM 255
SWARTZ
  Jacp196
  S. T. 248
  William 107
SWARZ
  S. T. 249
SWEAT
  James 255

SWEENEY
  Charles 214
  John 129, 157
  Thomas 214
SWEENY
  Byron 144
SWEET
  Frank 166
SWEETER
  Wallace 163
SWIFT
  Abram 169
  H. C. 64, 108
  Henry 53
  Isaac 77
  John 17, 55, 114
  Joseph 75
  Marcus 122
  Moses 166
  Philetus 35, 37, 49, 51-2, 130, 164, 168
SWIFT & JONES 107
SWIFT MILL 166
SWORDS
  T. & J. 66
SYELBACK
  Henry 186
SYKES 91, 92
SYMONDS
  Amos 227
  William 234

T

TABOR
  Warren 245
TAFT 210, 219
  Aaron 218
  B. C. 219
  Bazaleel 49
  C. 216
  Chapin 219
  Hannah 225
  Jesse 219
  Josiah 219
  Myron 219, 221, 224
  Robert 18, 216, 219
TAGGART 232
  Samuel 232
TAINTER 210
  Jesse 210
TALBOT
  Samuel 33, 203
TALCOTT
  Daniel 192
TALCOTT & BATTY 192
TALLEYRAND 225
TALLMADGE
  Samuel 201
TALLMAN 263
  Clarissa 148
  E. B. 145
  Elizabeth 148
  James 148
  John 148, 149
  Thomas 145
TANNER 67
TAPPAN 127
  William 135-6
TAYLOR 44, 83-5, 97, 112, 118, 218
  Aaron 207
  B. F. 127
  Benjamin 223
  Charles 108

TAYLOR (cont.)
  Clinton 213, 222
  Daniel 239
  Dolly 29
  Dorothy 112
  E. 38, 52
  Edward 175, 225
  Elder 169
  Elijah 207
  Eliphalet 52, 109, 116
  Ezekiel 107
  George 131
  Henry 51, 103, 107, 112, 175
  J. & D. 104
  J. W. 212
  James 186, 195, 267
  Janna 245
  John 12, 62, 204, 207, 212, 239
  Loring 223
  Minerva 29
  Myron 187
  Othniel 17, 34, 112, 114, 262
  Otho 63
  Phineas 198
  Rachel 212
  Richard 95, 142
  Robert 83. 97
  Ruel 175
  T. Byron 175
  Thomas 187
  William 119
TAYLOR'S HOTEL 55, 103
TEACHOUT
  Alonzo 182
  Oscar 187
TEELEY
  Edward 212
TEFFT
  B. F. 64, 66
TELFORD
  Francis 142
  George 142
TELLER
  Isaac 169
TEMPLE
  A. B. 149
  Daniel 169
TENNEY
  Martin 266
  Oliver 262-3
  Solomon 267
TENNY
  M. 266
TENNY SCHOOLHOUSE 266
TERRELL
  John 106
TERRY
  Abram 122, 213, 268
  Betsey 30
  James 266
  John 268
TERWILLAGER 89
TYALER
  J. 108
THATCHER
  Elisha 159
  Israel 159
  James 258
  John 159
  Julia 151
  Solomon 161
  Stephen 159, 161
THAYENDENEGA 127
THAYER 217

THAYER (cont.)
  Alfred 256
  Charles 158
  D. 208
  Henry 124, 246
  Joel 165
  Levi 165
  Oscar 122
  Preston 256
  Reuben 78
  Samuel 112
  Silas 202
  Sylvanus 19, 216–7
THAYER FARM 114
THOMAS 159, 262
  Anna 246
  Anna Abbey 246
  David 210, 246
  Frank 269
  George 60, 180, 246
  Henry 187
  James 116–7
  John 104, 203
  Joseph 144
  Lowell 246
  Lucy 246
  Malvina 246
  Mark 175
  Mary 246
  N. W. 241
  Nathan 246
  Olive 246
  Peter 130
  Richard 191
  S. M. 169
  Sally 246
  Samuel 205
  Wm. f-96, 182, 246
  Zimri 246
THOMAS' MILL 206
THOMPSON 19, 24, 38–9, 104, 219
  Airy 39
  & Benedict 104
  & Cook 155
  David 229
  F. F. 66, 107
  Firman 257
  Francis 175
  Franshay 187
  Geoerge 187, 210
  Henley 255
  Henry 96
  Ira 108
  John 142, 147, 161
  Joseph 187
  L. P. & Company 166
  M. L. P. 64, 112
  Melvin 123
  Otis 218, 219
  Reuben 255
  Samuel 112, 122
  T. M. 110
  Thaddeus 162
  William 234
THORN
  Chester 182
THORNTON
  Alexander 142, 175
  Amos 256
  John 144
THORPE
  Henry 258–9
  William 255, 259

THRALL
  Joseph 202
  L. G. 264
THROOP
  Azel (Asel) f-176, 178, 180–1, 188
  Benjamin 178, 181, 188
  Fanny Van Dusen 188
  J. A. 178
  Joseph 186
  Rachel 178, 188
THROOPS 178
THURBER
  Amaziah 251
  Henry 267
  William 251
THURBUR 160
TIBBALS
  Albert 259–60
  David 256, 259
  Noah 256
  Peter 256
TIBBALS FARM 256
TICHNOR'S POINT 119
TICKNER
  H. 166
TIERNEY
  Owen 187
TIERNY
  James 162
TIFFANY 44, 180, 221
  Alexander 66
  Beals & Johnson 104
  Byron 240
  Edmond 115
  F. J. 115
  Francis 115
  Horace 246
  Isaiah 182
  John 182
  L. 227
  Olney 115
  Susannah 115
  Sylvester 53, 66, 102, 106
  Zachariah 115
TIFFANY'S 208
TIFT
  Amasa 264
TILDEN
  Christopher 187
  William 187
TILLATSON
  Elijah 104
TILLMAN
  Andrew 130, 136
  S. D. 77
  William 129, 136
TILLOTSON 106
  Elijah 118
  L. H. f-107
  Levi 107, 108
  Lorenzo 117, 119, 125
  O. 118
  Ruth f-74
  Wilbur 122
TIMENS
  John 132
TIMMERMAN
  B. F. 199
TIMMON
  William 123
TINLINE
  Elizabeth 135
TINNEY
  Madison 175

TINNEY (cont.)
  Martha 235
TIPPETS
  William 128, 130
TIPPETTS
  Elizabeth 144
  Stephen 144
  William 69, 128
TISDALE
  Minerva 236
TITUS
  Anson 166
  Billy 175
  C. M. 58
  Oliver 175
  S. W. 113
TOBEY
  F. B. 208
  F. N. 209, f-215
  Lyman 264
  William 269
TOBY
  Benjamin 214
  F. N. 214
  Frederick 212
  Robert 266
TOCKER
  Manly 170
TOLE
  George 175
TOLL
  David 142
TOLMAN
  J. N. 113
  Ward 242
TOMPKINS 44
  Armstrong 155
  Daniel 69
  Seaman 156
TOMPKINSON
  J. 108, 169
TOOKER 221
  M. 132
  Manly 113, 181
  Orin 144
  Samuel 132
TOOMEY
  Jeremiah 213
  Timothy 213
TOPLIFF
  Zilpha 30
TOPPING
  Reed 148
  Samuel 149
TORRANCE 146
  G. W. 200
  Samuel 240
  Sheldon 240
TORREY 41
  Augustus 63
  Harry 264
  Hiram 136
  Paul 37
  S. H. 53
  Samuel 52, 80, 108, 153, 263, 264
TORRY
  William 112
TORRY'S COAL YARD 102
TOTMAN
  Ashael 222
  L. W. 239
  Levi 245
TOUHEY
  John 123

TOUSEY
  Thomas 132
TOUT
  J. 169
  John 166
  W. C. 166
TOWER 84
  David 113
  Philo 156
TOWLER
  John 75-6
TOWN 105
  Reuben 108
TOWNS
  Ichabod 201
TOWNSEND
  Adrian 157, 161
  Carolyn 235
  E. G. 113, 170
  Edwin 175
  George 235
  H. 82-a
  Henry 55, 123
  Hezekiah 122
  Kneeland 203
  Mary 148
  Peter 109
  Thomas 161
  William 53, 58, 122
TOZER
  Edward 266
  Robert 251
  S. A. 109
TRACEY
  W. C. 208
TRACEY HOUSE 104
TRACHOUT
  Alonzo 161
TRACY
  Abel 160
  Joshua 105
  Peter 124
TRAFTON
  George 245
  Henry 240
  John 240
TRALL
  Joseph 200
TRAPULL
  Frederick 143
TRASK 207
  Lyman 124
  Mary 212
TRAVIS
  [illegible]on 157
  Rufus 243, 245
TREAT
  Albert 240
  Daniel 152
  Richard 251
TREMBLY
  John 120, 247
  Israel 258
  Isaac 249, 251
  Rev. 259
TRENFIELD
  P. 190
  Peter 190
TRICKEY
  Stephen 120
TRIMMER
  Charles 255
TRISLER
  John 166

TROUP 71
  Robert 31-2, 49, 61, 68, 136
TROWBRIDGE 221
TRUMAN 234
  Whiting 119
TUBBS 210, 229
  Harold 245
  Henry 245
  James 231
  Luther 246
  Seth 227, 240
TUBBS & CO. STORE 210
TUCKER 257
  Abner 43
  Benjamin 257
  Caroline 257
  Ephraim 257-8
  Eugene 187
  James 221
  Jerome 257
  Manly 182
  Minerva 257
TUCKERMAN 228
TUFFS
  John 152
  Thomas 152
TULFORD
  William 214
TUPPER
  Elihu 115
  Smith 143
TURK
  Frederick 144
TURNBULL
  Adam 147
  Alexander 147, 149
  Edward 147
TURNER 66, 202, 209, f-235
  David 187, 195
  Ephraim 209, 229
  George 142, 155
  James 153
  John 199
  N. 199
  Nathaniel 202
  Noah 187
  Peter 198-9, 202-3
  Roswell 19, 24, 227, 230-1
  Solomon 199, 202
  Spencer 142
  Thomas 197, 198
  William 199
TUTTLE 119, 248, 250
  Ashbael 118
  Benjamin 148
  Henry 120, 123
  J. K. 113
  Jared 18, 247-8
  Jay 251
  M. 266
  Thomas 119
TWOHEY
  Jerry 121
  Martin 187
TYLER 76, 83, 231, 242
  Comfort 14, 25, 30
  E. G. 59
  Edward 59, 76, 112
  Edwin 267
  John 39
  Nathan 263
  W. C. 142
  William 263

TYLOR
  Lydia 30
TYRRELL
  Joseph 119

U

UNDERHILL 129
  Charles 107, 111
  Henry 122
  James 144
  P. B. 64, 107, 111
  Punderson 41, 110-1
  Robert 156
  & Seymour 102
UPHAM 76
  Hannah 76, 106
UPJOHN, MESSRS. & SON 75
UPTON
  James 200, 202-3
  Josiah 200
URBER
  George 124
UTLEY
  William 116, 256
UTTEL
  Hiram 157
UTTER
  Joseph 255

V

VAIL 136
  Charles 76
  J. P. 133
  John 144
VAILDE
  John 144
VALENTINE
  John 222
  S. 201
  Samuel f-94
VAN ALLSTYNE
  George 132
VAN ALSTYNE
  George 113, 170
VAN ANTWERP
  Isaac 157
VANARSDALE 134
  C. C. 134
  J. R. 134-5
VAN ARSDEL
  J. W. 155
VAN AUKEN 129
  George 175
  Theron 167
VAN AUTRICK 258
VAN BENSCHOTEN
  Henry 212
  M. 212
VAN BERGER
  E. 142
VAN BRANKEN
  "Old Uncle" 153
VAN BUREN
  Charles 187
  George 162
  Jeremiah 175
  Martin 154, 235
  Thomas 90
VAN BUREN'S LIGHT INF. 90

VANCE
David 32
VAN CLIVE
Edward 66
VAN COTT 205
VAN DE CARR
David 120, 187
VANDECUR
David 162
VANDEMARK
Joseph 165
Lodowick 165
Ross & Cooley 166
VANDENBURG
P. S. 115
VANDERHOOF 179
Abram 178, 179
F. D. 64
Garret 177
Grazilla 30
James 175, 175
Jacob 177
John 177
William 175
VAN DER VEEN
C. 135
VANDERVORT
C. 166
VANDEUSEN
George 175
Henry 175
Robert 175
VAN DEUSEN
Rebecca 30
VANDEVERE 256
VANDEVORT
Ella f-172
Thomas f-172
VAN DUSEN 132
Ambrose 52-3
Fanny 188
Henry 187
William 110
VAN DUSEY
H. L. 182
VAN DUYNE
George 175
William 175
VAN DUZEN
A. L. 182
William 192
VAN DYKE 12
VAN DYNE
George 187
VAN FLEET
Joshua 51-2, 176-7, 180-1, 193
VAN FOSSEN
Isaac 239
John 53
VAN GELD
Charles 187
VAN GELDER 142, 145
A. 161
Abram 148
Alfred 144
Amelia 150
Beekman 149
Burt 149
Catharine 148
Charles 144
Henry 142
Martha 150
Peter 145

VAN GORDER
William 175
VAN HORN 44
Gilbert 144
VAN HOUTEN
James 142
VAN KUREN
Isaac 175
Simon 175
William 175
VAN NESS 24, 38, 249
VANNESS
Charles 156
Henry 205
VAN NEST 134
Abraham 134
VAN NESTE
George 134
VAN NORMAN
Silas 214
VAN NOSTRAND
Isaac 151
Julia 151
VAN ORMAN 119
Aaron 241
Eliza 118
Isaac 60, 118
Jesse 118
John 115
Joseph 117, 118
VAN ORSDALE
Aduck 144
VAN OSDOL 147
VAN OSTRAN
Isaac f-148
J. A. f-148
Julia f-148
VAN OSTRAND
Abraham 144
VAN OSTRANDER
William 144
VAN PETTEN 95
VAN RENSSELAER 75
J. 105
Maunsell 75
Philip 45
Stephen 45
VANSICE
Jno. 66
VAN SICKLE
G. f-179, 179
VAN SLYKE
George 144
J. K. 132
VANTASSEL
Samuel 39
VAN TOPEN
John 52
VAN VALKENBURG 67
VAN VLECK
James 191
VAN VOLKENBURG
William 170
VAN VORHIS
H. 201
VAN WERT
John 158
VAN WINKLE
Edwin 175
VAN WIRT
William 32
VAN WORMER
Albert 175
Edwin 175

VAN WORMER (cont.)
Michael 30
VAN ZANDT
John 142
VARNEY
G. A. 216
VARTIE
Thomas 147
VARY
Harriet 214
VEADER
John 133
VEAIN
Charles 144
VEDDER 57
Harlo 161
VEEDER
John 109
VEGESACK 84
VENDEMARK
Frederick 166
VENDERHOOF
F. 166
VER PLANCK 71-2, 129
Gulian 70
S. H. 58
Samuel 129
VICKEREY
Martin 187
VICKERY
Nelson 187
Robert 264
Theodore 187
VICKORY
Franklin 268
VIDLINE
William 142
VIEUN
John 142
VINAL 229, 230
VINCENT 91
Charles 175
Eugene 144
J. Wheelock 239
Mortimer 246
Thomas 239, 241
VINGH
James 144
VINTON 121
VOAK
J. B. 113
VOGD
Abram 222
VOORHEES
H. V. 134
Henry 134
William 128
VORCE
William 156
VORREUTER
Simon 105
VOSBURG
Abraham 53
Barney 175
L. 147
VOSBURGH
Albert 204
VOTTLEY
Charles 168
VOTY
Elder 169
VROOMAN 57, 77
Bart. 57
Matilda 150

VROOMAN (cont.)
William 77, 78

W

WACK
C. P. 134
WADE 220
Elisha 61, 220
J. M. 168
WADER
Charles 168
J. A. 168
Jacob 53
WADHAUS
Mortimer 201
WADSWORTH 24, 44, 48, 54
Gad 78
James 14, 16, 24, 39, 78, 160
Jeremiah 24
William 24, 37, 44, 49
WAGER
Benjamin 221
WAGGENER
David 15
WAGNER
Casper 144
WAGONER 59
WAGSTAFF & RIFFORD 114
WAINWRIGHT
E. 109
WAIT
Lorin 217
WAITE
B. G. 257
Benjamin 257, 259
D. Byron 253, 259
Edwin 257
Ezra 52, 218
Green 257, 259
H. 256
Nelson 257
Thomas 257
WAKEMAN
John 57
WALBRIDGE
Hiram 130
WAL BRIDGE
Stephen 259
WALBUR
T. 129
WALCH 147
WALCOT
John 163
WALDEN 44
WALDO 256
WALDRON
Benjamin 106–7, 109, 241
Charles 240
Nathan 18, 209
Richmond 228
WALES
Arvine 268
enry 143
Mary 246
Samuel 268
WALKER 35, 83, 227, 210, 255, 258–9
Ansen 116
Benjamin 101
Betsey 254
Caleb 102
Calvin 83, 130, 144
Eli 60

WALKER (cont.)
Eliakim 240
George 196
Gideon 254
Henson 180
James 175
John 205, 254
Mary 212
Nathaniel 194
Pitts 249, 258
Richard 255–6
Robert 107
Sarah 179
Tinsdel 240
William 13, 17, 198
WALL
Lott 175
WALLACE
Ira 187
James 133
WALLING
George 204
James 199, 204
Levi 257
Peter 258
WALLIS 34, 102, 109
WALSH
D. 127
M. 116
WALTHART
J. 169
WALTHER
Phillip 156
WALTON
George 158
WANACONG
David 268
WANNALL
Thomas 234
WARD 38, 66, 118, 120, 148, 257
A. H. 219
Andrew 19, 255, 259
C. B. 118, 119
Calvin 227
Harry 227
Ichabod 178
Jabez 257
Jackson 162
Jerry 259
John 202
Moses 36–7, 118–9
Nancy 256
Robert 124
S. C. 64
Samuel 66
Shadrach 256, 259
Stephen 117, 119
William 122, 202, 233, 255–7
WARDEN
Chauncey 251,
Henry 144
Lyman 251
WARE
Henry 144
Joseph 118
WARIS
Moses 157
WARFIELD
Alexander 175
Andrew 124
Arnold 180
Elvira 182
Eugene 162
Evan 180

WARFIELD (cont.)
George 187
Leonard 182
Nathan 180
Newton 144
Richard 233
Thomas 180, 182
William 53, 116, f-196
WARN 176
WARNER
A. C. 142
A. J. 77, 175
Asahel 49, 52, 58
Asel 175
Charles 169
Chloe 167
Daniel 160
George 108
J. 219
Jesse 164, 168
John 164, 175
Lewis 169
Lucinda 169
Mark 169
Martin 169
Mary 169
Matthew 49, 52, 58
Milton 160
Oliver 160, 169
Orrin 185
Rufus 160
Sally 49
Samuel 128, 148
Solomon 40, 148
Ulysses 52–3
Warren 175
William 182, 228, 231
WARNERS
Edwin 182
WARRELLS 241
WARREN 44, 100
Abigail 112
Abijah 61, 232, 240–1, 251
Daniel 18, 159
Elijah 104
Elizabeth f-235
General 92
John 79, 154
Russell 159
William 120
WARRICK
Freeman 255
WARTH
Smuel f-140
WASHBURN 104
Alvin 255
Benjamin 152
Chester 253
Clarissa 253
Ebenezer 157
Gail 263
George 266
Ira 267
Joshua 153
Seth 202
Valentine 234
WASHINGTON 11–2, 16, 23, 124, 136, 239, 217
WASHINGTON HOTEL 104
WATCH
Moses 158
WATE
James 143

WATERBURY
    C. 204
WATERFORD 83
WATERMAN 68
    Anson 167
    Charles 264
WATERS
    Cassie 192
    Jonathan 257, 259
    Stephen 144
    Willis 257
WATERS & COOK 192
WATKINS
    Abraham 155
    Alanson 49
    Charles 267
    Clinton 160
    Isaac 37, 262-3
    John 166
    Levi 264
    Lydia 264
    Mark 264
    Nathan 18, 261-4
    Samuel 264
    Sarah 264
    Stephenn 18
    Susannah 264
    Thankful 35, 262
    William 18, 261-4
WATROUS
    George 234
    Henry 264
    Myron 233
WATSON 103
    Charles 98
    Elkanah 18, 66, 103, 127
    Leancourt 25
    W. W. 136
    William 130, 133
WATTERY
    Levi 156
WATTEWORTH
    J. C. 142
WATTS
    George 124
    Jonathan 212
WAY 228
WAYLAND
    John 111, 124
WAYNE 180
    Anthony 22, 23
    John 162
    William 65
WEAGH
    Conrad 175
WEATHERWAX
    David 122
    Levi 124
WEAVER
    T. Leslie 156
    Theo. 109
WEBB
    Charles 221
    Ezekiel 165
    Frederick 175
    George 223
    Homer 223
    William 204, 113
WEBER
    John 211
WEBSTER 75, 168
    D. C. 210
    D. F. 53
    Daniel 213

WEBSTER (cont.)
    Ephraim 25
    Horace 74, 75
    Huldah 30
    Isaac 49, 119
    Israel 146
    John 193
    Lester 146
    T. 210
    Uriah 217
    Willard 146
WEBSTER HOUSE 104-5
WEED
    Eber 257-8
WEEKS
    Smith 33, 60
WEISENBECK
    E. 105, 109
WEISS
    Martin 175
WEITZEL 95, 96
WELCH 212
    Daniel 256
    Elias 258
    George 234
    John 200, 205
    Margaret 255
    Peter 254-6
WELLEMEYER
    John 186
WELLER
    Charles 118
    Henry 162
    John 158
WELLES
    Henry 39
    William 59, 169
WELLS 17, 38, 118, 99
    Ananias 59
    Benjamin 34-5, 63, 102, 111, 159
    Charles 97
    Cromwell 181
    Cyrus 225, 257, 231-2
    Deacon 220
    E. 261, 264
    Ebenezer 190
    J. 256
    J. K. 38
    John 180
    Jonathan 111
    Joseph 190
    Laban 181, 187
    Manning 111
    Marcellus 222
    Moses 81
    Richard 41, 63-4, 107-8, 111
    Walter 160
WELLMAN 88
WELSH
    John 144
    T. 115
WELTON 259
    Alanson 111, 232
    C. B. 108
    Orsel 213
    Titus 232
WEMET
    Charles 257
WEMETT
    Alonzo 259
    Andrew 257
    Henry 53, 259, 260
    Joseph 256, 259-60
    Melford 259

WEMMETT
    Joseph 269
WEMPLE 12
WENDELL
    Josiah 216
WENDLE
    Josiah 216
WENTER
    Jacob 124
WESLEY
    John 144
WESSELS 89
WEST 169
    A. T. 232
    Alvin 59
    Betsey 169
    Elbridge 187
    G. R. 108
    J. B. 231
    Jonathan 203
    L. W. 231
    Nathan 242
    William 234, 263
WESTBROOK
    Charles 268
    F. 255
    Frederick 255, 259
    Isaac 257, 268
    Jesse 258
    Richard 154
    William 255
WESTFALL
    Alfred 144
    Cornelius 165, 168
    Elias 259
    James 259-60
    John 255
    William 187
WESTFIELD
    George 144
WESTHERD
    Charles 175
WESTON
    C. F. 169
    Charles 124
    Ira 108
WESTOON
    Edwin 124
WESTOVER 205
WETMORE
    E. B. 233
    Elam 259-60
    O. 259
    Orlando 256
    P. 259
    Prosper 81
    Robert 110
WEYERSBURG
    Carl 187
WHALLEY 34, 36, 104, 109
WHALLING'S STORE 59
WHALON
    John 196
WHEADON
    Sela 147
WHEAT
    C. 77, 130
    Congdon 58
    Corydon 77-8, 130
    Franklin 187
    V. B. 175
WHEATLEY 257
    James 224

WHEATON
Benjamin 144
David 244
Polly 242
Samuel 34
WHEEDON
George 148
Samuel 148
WHEELER 168, 214–5, 241, 264, 266
A. 136
A. S. 142
Aaron 240, 246
Alonzo 187
Anson 53
Aurelius 187
Beman 40
Benjamin 117, 210, 213–5, 235
Betsey 212
C. 203
Charles 81, 90–1, 122, 142, 233
Chloe 246
Cyrus 241
Edgar 175
Eli 169
Elijah 227
George 118
Isaac 200
J. M. 57, 110
John 19, 210, 230, 256
Jonas 53
Martin 170, 212
Milton 121
Rial 187
S. R. 40, f-206, 215, 238
Samuel 214, 250
Simeon 53, 210, 215
Sylvester 227, 230
T. 30
Ulysses 74
Zenas 166
WHEELOCK
R. 219
Royal 219
WHELOCK
Alden 257
WHELPTON 42
WHIPPLE
Calvin 192
Daniel 142, 157
Henry 196
J. 142
Russel 115–6
Samuel 180
Walter 192
WHISKER
Robert 234
WHITAKER
Eli 142
Mary 148
S. 149
Stephen 149
WHITBECK 166, 257
Jacob 257
WHITCHER
Stephen 148
WHITCOMB 144
Thomas 203
Walter 108
WHITE 218, 264
Abel 60
Artemus 175
Charles 175
D. & Company 166
Daniel 14, 49, 154

WHITE (cont.)
David 52
Edward 129
Eunice 30
Frank 144
Fresbee & Company 166
George 175
Harley 255, 258
Hugh 14
Ira 70
J. J. 228
Jacob 177
James 63
John 149, 166
LaFayette 259
Lucian 124
M. 108
Oliver 207
T. F. 112
Thomas 148
WHITEHEAD
James 124
William 175
WHITEWATER & JACKSON 106
WHITING 77, 129
Bemis & Co. 104
Bowen 39, 45, 51–3, 73, 77, 130, 133
Edward 223
John 53
Theodore 224
W. M. 166
WHITMAN
Samuel 155
WHITMARSH
John 239
Rufus 240
WHITMORE 36, 165
Luke 148
Moses 167
O. 148
Oliver 34, 39, 132, 147, 148
Wells 36, 49, 148, 165–6
WHITNEY 145
Amelia 150
Ami f-67, 145–6, 148
Anna 150
Augustus 66
Bascom 40
Byram 148
Byron 150
Charles 187
Cheeney 145, f-150, 150
Clara 148
Clarissa 150
Columbus 148, 149
Cornelia 150
Daniel 150
Dennis 232
Dolly 150
George 66, 150, 187
Hachaliah 149–50
Hannah 150, f-150
Harriet 150
Hiram 187, 234
Isaac 261, 263
J. J. 82, 159
Jefferson 53
Joel 39, 146, 148, 246
Jonas 160
Jonathan 18, 39, 145, 150
Julia 148
Leonard 113
Luther 30, 145, 150, f-150
Lyman 232

WHITNEY (cont.)
May 150
Martha 150
Mary 150
Matilda 150
N. 52
Nathan 39, 145, 147–8, 246
Olive 145, f-150
Otis 145–6, 149
Peter 263
R. C. 146
Samuel 232
Sidney 150
Silas 225, 231
Sophronia 150
Susan 159
Sybil 148
Tacy 150
Temperance 148
W. A. 144
William 175
WHITNEY FAMILY 145
WHITTAKER
Halsey 258–9
John 257
WHITTERIE
Robert 154
WHITTLESEY 76
George 66
WHITTUM
James 175
John 175
WHITWELL
John 53
Stephen 124
WHORRALL
Ellen f-126
James f-126
WIBORN
Leroy 232
WICKAM
George 109
WICKHAM
John 53, 78
WICKS 118
J. 257
William 154
WIDENER 24
WIDMAN
A. 109
WIER
Peter 187
WILBER
Jno. 268
L. D. 166
P. 268
Samuel 268
Theron 268
WILBUR
B. 200
C. H. 119
George 157
James 175
John 175
L. F. 64
Leonidas 231
Samuel 160
T. 127
Thomas 135
William 175
WILBUR'S STORE 119
WILCOX 63, 100, 102, 206, 208
Abigail 214
Almira 214

WILCOX (cont.)
  Benjamin 250
  Charles 262–3
  Elmer 213
  Elnathan 34, 208, 211
  Enoch 208, 211
  Ezra 221
  Frank 213
  Franklin 89
  Frederick 213
  Hazzard 250
  I. W. 250
  Jairus 204
  Jared 52
  L. 64, 113–4
  Lucius 59, 64, 66, 102–3
  Minta 208
  Nancy 211
  Nathan 208
  Orson 126
  Ralph 208, 214
  Roswell 43
  Sally 263
  Terrissa Cooley 126
  Thomas 233
  Tilo:144
  Walter 234
WILDER 18, 24, 102, 146, 189, 218, 241, 247–8, 251
  Anna 188
  Asa 247, 248
  Augustus 81, 251
  Daniel 238, 247, 248, 249
  Elijah 132, 148
  Ephraim 17, 114, 239, 241, 250, 262
  G. 248, 250
  Gamaliel 17, 25, 176, 228, 238–41, 247, 250
  George 250
  Ira 91, 116–7, 121
  J. 200, 248
  J. H. 146
  James 248
  John 239
  Jonas 240, 247
  Jonathan 116, 132
  Joseph 247
  Lucy 248
  Lydia 241
  N. G. 188
  Orpha 249
  Timothy 239, 241
  Wallace 251
WILDER'S MILL 189
WILDS 257
  Derby 256, 259
  Eliza 254
WILEY 134–5, 201
  A. 257
  Abram 227, 235, 256, 257
  Charles 134
  Lena 266
  Robert 35, 263
  William 264
WILKINS
  Andrew 113
  Thomas 144, 175
WILKINSON
  Jemima 103
  Jeremiah 15, 25
WILLARD 91, 132
  Samuel 132
WILLER
  William 168

WILLETS
  Samuel 194
WILLETT
  Marinus 209
WILLIARD
  Urana 202
WILLIAMS 17, 67, 89, 128, 166, 170, 241, 249, 257
  Abijah 198, 202–4
  Betsey 112
  Charles 187, 196
  David 249
  Davis 182
  Ebenezer 117
  Elisha 35, 202
  Frank 179
  G. N. 59
  George 53, 59, 121, 157
  Henry 158, 162
  James 97, 198
  Joab 231
  Job 219
  John 111, 144, 234
  Joseph 212
  Lucinda 198
  Lyman 166
  Millard 161
  Pelham 75
  Peter 181
  R. M. 56, 127
  & Remington 59
  Richard 136
  Robert 198
  S. 127
  Sanford 147, 148
  T. H. 115
  Thomas 118, 129, 227
  Timothy 202
  W. M. 218
  William 32, 38, 79, 102, 112
WILLIAMS SCHOOLHOUSE 259
WILLIAMSON 22, 30, 32, 35, 55, 127
  Charles 19–22, 31, 66, 78–9, 126, 129, 136, 178, 247
  John 144
WILLING 166
WILLIS
  Daniel 80
  Marshall 124
WILLISON
  Newlove 222
  William 221
WILLISTEN
  Seth 241
WILLISTON 264
  Seth 34, 203, 211
WILLOUGHBY
  George 175
WILLMARTH
  Asa 178
WILLS
  M. 115
  Richard 41
WILLSON 80, 110
  A. L. 180
  Augustus 179
  Electra f-235
  Frances Pierpont 235
  George 53, 79–80, 82, 110, 112, 182, 187
  Gilbert f-235
  Henry 81, 187
  J. 41
  Jared 38–9, 52, 58, 76, 80, 108
  John 255

WILLSON (cont.)
  Marcius 80–1, f-235, 235
  Nathaniel f-235
  Robert 255
  Selecta f-235
  Thomas 232
  Turner f-235
  William 255
WILLSON'S HISTORIES 81
WILLSON'S READERS 81
WILLYS
  David 213
WILMARTH
  Asa 190, 193
  Ezra 198, 201–2, 204
  Gersham 202
  James 201
  Mary 202
  Otis 200
WILSON 24, 66, 99, 159, 203, 232
  & Allen 176, 178, 179
  A. G. 231
  A. L. 166
  Alphonso 142
  Andrew 149, 157
  Benjamin 208
  Chapin 108
  David 52–3, 130, 147, 194
  E. A. 142
  Elder 34, 211
  Ezekiel 254
  Ezra 144
  Franklin 214
  Frederick 254
  George 66, 122, 157, 165
  Harvey 157, 267
  Hiram 157
  Isaac 195
  J. C. 147
  J. H. 231
  James 132
  Jane f-146
  Jared 37, 51–2, 57, 167
  Jerry 234, 237
  Jno. 233
  John 19, 67, 130, 142, 144, f-146, 148–9, 203, 232, 254, 266
  Joseph 163
  Katy 254
  Lewis 250
  Nathaniel 166
  Robert 163
  Sarah f-146
  & Stokely 154
  Sylvester 113
  T. F. f-152, 148
  Thomas 163, 175, 226
  Timothy 200
  W. D. 169
  William 75, 109, 122, 147, 149, 156, 257, 267
WILTER
  Austin 157
  William 157
WILTS;159
WIMPLE
  Philia;237
WINCH
  Amasa;257
  John;255, 257–9
WINCHESTER
  E. C.;242
WINDSOR
  Matthew;192

WINEGAR
  Edwin 222
WINFIELD
  Henry 255
  Horace 258
  John 255
  Joseph 258
  W. 256
WING
  John 255, 256, 259
  & Nelson 165
  Samuel 266
WINSHIP
  Cyrus 256
WINSLOW 210
  Hubbard 132
WINTER
  Aaron 142
  M. J. 213
WINTERS
  Thomas 187
WIRE FARM 119
WIRMAN
  Michael 175
  Mike 144
WIRNETT
  Milford 234
WIRTS
  Helen 167, 168
WISE
  Abigail 155
WISEMAN
  William 255
WISEWELL
  Charles 268
  Frank 81
  H. F. 262
WISNER
  H. 156
  J. T. 190, 266
  James 112
  Jehiel 34, 168
  P. B. 127
  Polydor 69, 128–9, 136
WISTAR'S BRIGADE 93
WISTER 102
WISTNER
  Jacob 187
WITHERNELL
  John 203
  Jno. 205
WITTELS
  William 121
WITTER 79
  Alfred 166
  Austin 124
  Ezra 79
  Hiram 124
  W. B. 40
  Warren 53
WITTERMAUTTE
  Jno. 124
WIZNER
  P. B. 64
WODER
  Jacob 169
WOHLZEMUTH
  William 203
WOLCOTT 258
  E. 241
  Horatio 108
  Jno. 124
  Oliver 12
  William 175

WOLF
  A. B. 142
WOLFIN
  Levi 30
WOLSEY
  Polly 169
WOLVERTON
  Charles 142
  Job 124
WOLVIN
  Alonzo 175
  William 175
WOOD 48
  A. A. 112
  A. Augustus 132
  Ann 135
  B. B. 217
  C. H. 218
  Carlton 53
  Charles 123, 142
  E. F. 248
  Elizabeth 135
  Ezra 148
  Francix 182
  Frank 249
  Hiram 267
  Isaac 194, 248
  J. G. 249
  J. M. 147
  James 152, 153, 154
  Jerome 163
  Job 229, 230
  John 119, 132, 147, 175, 223, 248–9
  Keziah 249
  L. B. 113
  Levi 60
  Lorenzo 121
  Nathaniel 251
  Ralph 135
  Randall f-253
  Richard 205
  Samuel 113
  Stephen 110
  Thomas 135
  Walter 211
  William 38, 57, 64, 107, 110, 160, 192, 249
WOODARD
  David 168
  Jas 113
WOODBURY 86
WOODCOCK
  Harrison 144, 175
  Harry 242
WOODHULL
  Joseph 167
WOODIN 160
  James 175
WOODRUFF 160
  Charles 116–7, 144
  H. E. 160
  J. L. 108
  Jacob 105
  Jeremiah 242
  Louis 144
  Orange 17
  Solomon 230, 231
  W. D. 168
  W. G. 195
  William 166
WOODS 217, 221
  E. S. 216
  H. C. 232
  James 52

WOODS (cont.)
  John 69, 128, 136
  Samuel 120
WOODWARD 115
  Asa 40
  David 148
  M. 250
  Sarah 152
WOODWORTH
  E. B. 147
  Erastus 63
  Frederick 190
  Nestor 58
  Philo 203, 221
WOOL 90
WOOLCUTE
  William 144
WOOLEDGE 218
WOOLSEY
  George 187
WOOLSTEN
  Mark 123
WOOLSTON
  Barzilia 201
  G. 208
  Joseph 201
  William 201
WORDEN 249
  Alvah 51–2
  Clark 249
  Joseph 187
  L. G. 255, 258
  Marvin 251
  Squire 251
WORTH
  John 112
WORTHINGTON
  Ambrose 104
WORTHLY
  Austin 144
WORTHY
  M. P. 64, 231
  Merian 234
WORDEN
  M. 266
WRIDE
  John 32
WRIGHT f-80, 229, 259
  Abijah 60, 228, 230, 258
  Charles 143, 175
  D. 108
  E. M. 233
  Elias 218, 219
  George 58
  Isaac 233–4, 256
  James 230
  John 175
  Lester 161
  Richard 113, 144, 169, 230
  Russell 162, 187
  Simeon 251
  Thomas 60, 169, 200, 203
  William 51, 225, 226
WUILSEHTEGGER
  John 144
WUN-NUT-HAT 9
WYATT
  John 180
WYCKMAN 21
WYCKOFF
  J. V. D. 166
  James 162
  Watson 120, 161
  William 113

WYMAN
  H. K.   166
WYNCOOP
  Peter   145
WYOLL
  William   109
WYRD
  Thomas   122
WYVILL
  W. M.   108
WYVILLE
  Thomas   108

Y

YAN
  Edwin   266
  Joel   266
YARKER
  Percel   163
YATES   133
  Andrew   133
  Solomon   39
YECKLEY
  J. A.   156
  Jno.   157
  John   148–9

YEOMANS
  Emerson   185
  Moses   142
  Nathaniel   242
YONNONDIO   10
YORK   160
  Walter   158
YORKS   259
YOST
  Joseph   258
YOUNG   67
  Aaron   53, 71, 130
  Abraham   152, 156
  Ambrose   196
  Andrew   246
  Anson   149
  Brigham   117, 201
  Charles   142
  Cornelius   124
  Edward   213
  Henry   157
  Isaac   162
  J. C.   142
  Jacob   152
  James   195
  John   190
  Moses   132
  William   32, 182

YOUNGER
  Judge   38
YOUNGLOVE
  Aaron   41, 52
  Elihu   29
  Elisha   107
  L.   102
  Timothy   102, 107
YOUNGS   257
  H. E.   f-148, 150
  H. L.   f-148
  Israel   149
  James   187
  John   157
  M.   f-148

Z

ZABRISKIE
  F. N.   135
ZEIKE
  A. S.   81
ZOPP
  George   144